1

Recently by Marcus Sanford

Cataclysm Geology signage

Titles at Amazon

Most recent:

MANSFELDER FREIHEIT!   *Can a young constitutional state survive an impetuous prince?*

The Enthroned King, His Kingdom, and Its Opponents

Early Acts and the West's Tailspin

To Hillsdale College,
A pure study of the civics
of the imperative kingdom.

Marcus Sanford

Jan. 2024

3

Thanks to Travis Cowan, Lynn Carmichael, Clyde Cowan

Also by Marcus Sanford
THE GOSPEL I NEVER KNEW. *Roman's mission in a PC age.*
MORE OF THE SAME (formerly DESOLATED at Amazon), novel
BE CAREFUL WHAT YOU WISH FOR, documentary background for MORE OF THE SAME
THE NERVE, novel, script
DELUGE OF SUSPICIONS, novel
WHAT IT SHOULD HAVE BEEN (formerly SENSELESS at Amazon), novel, script

www.interplans.net

Underlined chapter references exist because much of the material was copied from online forum format.

Contents:

Introduction 7
The Enthroned King 13
The Davidic References of Early Acts 43
The 40 Days 49
The Top Five Impacts of the Kingdom 59
The Reign of Christ in the Reformation Sense 63
Integrated NT History 77

Additional Features 109
The Strange Case of the Translation of Acts 3:21
How We Get Back To Meaning, a universal story
The 'Anothen' Realm
Background Resources

Introduction

"The Christ who was violently humiliated by Rome was 'back,' in Caesar's court, through Paul, unstoppable, telling him that Caesar existed to honor Christ!"

It seems that like Genesis 1, early *Acts* is somewhat 'precious' and guarded because it is the opening scenes of the church. Many have invested themselves in views about these things and whether true or not, they protect their view. People leave *Acts* and check many other passages. The odd thing about this is *Acts* is actual history unfolding, not conceptual. We can stay in the passage and see what *happened*. That is more effective communication.

Whether you have studied the Bible 25 days or 25 years, I think you will find some remarkable insights in this essay on *Acts*. Let me be more specific: whether your interest is the *Spirit*, or the *kingdom* or the *resurrection*, or

Israel and/or a millennium, I don't think you will have heard what is put forward here.

Three things are intended by this overall presentation: *1, to restore the Reformation sense of the reign of Christ, which resulted in the US saying it was 'a nation under God.'* Eisenhower added "under God" to the pledge when detecting how Communist philosophy was attacking the US immediately after the WW2. It was always implied.

2, to solidify the NT sense of proof of itself, and of its authority, through its statements about the destruction of Jerusalem at the end of the 'apostolic generation.'

3, to reinforce that apostolic teaching is sourced in the 40 days of Christ's teaching what the OT meant, not in a list of NT documents and letters decided upon many years later--although there is a lot of overlap.

Without these things, the church has three rather weak offerings: a largely ineffective kingdom—or something in the distant future, and a weakened resurrection that is merely on the level of any other miracle that took place; an almost non-existent use of the epic destruction of Israel in 66+ AD, as explained by the NT; a complicated way of settling the authority of the NT far removed from *events* of its times.

What we want to see is that there is an 'enthronement' package that will surge forward in history, until, by all accounts, you can say that the kingdom is established as planned, that it is an entity that is planted, never to be moved, and that its goal of being founded *in honor of* Christ for all ages is being met.

I'm not sure how, but I think I was started on this project by noticing something that was kind of the opposite of many people's interest in the resurrection. All the questions were about *what proved the resurrection?* The opposite of this would be *what did the resurrection prove?* At first I knew it was an important question, but I couldn't quite tell what the answer was—certainly not as easy as the other way around.

Finally, one day, I realized what the 'banner' verse of this essay was saying—that the resurrection was the enthronement of Christ, Acts 2:30, 31. I open the study with that.

You might find these explanations repetitive, but please bear with it. Somethings are intended to be repeated in light of the other astonishing statements of *Acts*.

Most of all, you will find this treatment to be inspiring and challenging. You might also call it *subversive*. There is a lot in the material that soars far above the 'God help me out of my situation' concerns. To actually present the enthroned Christ as the apostles did will 'turn the world upside down'--which wouldn't hurt! Please read with a new challenging question in the back of your mind: does the material answer Marxism?

9

In light of the positions and postures of the Biden administration of January 2021, if our pastors and believers do not come to terms with the NT picture of the enthroned Christ, Christians will not have a basis to challenge transformational Marxists in the US, and its faith will disappear. I mean the NT picture will disappear; like China, the US may still have 'allowed' churches. Those are the stakes.

Early *Acts* needs to be rescued from futurism and from subjectivity because both of these diminish our sense of the power of kingdom so badly. Believers should be warning neighbors and leaders not to ignore the Son, who will smash all enemies. I am astonished that what is the most demanding and challenging message of early *Acts* is almost non-existent and even opposed. Human nature moves toward cowardice.

This explanation of our current situation is written to rescue the West from its tailspin, and to provide solid meat to those who will find that what is 'allowed' by China Marxism is increasingly shallow when compared to the actual teachings of the apostles. It is already standard for some churches.

This kind of declaration to the public and its leaders needs the underpinning of two things to proceed confidently: the knowledge that the resurrection was the public enthronement of Christ as a King who summons to all people to live rightly; and the knowledge that Christ announced the destruction of Jerusalem 40 years in advance, in actual public history, as a warning to all people to 'pay homage to the Son.'

--*Marcus Sanford*
February 2021

1
THE ENTHRONED KING

The resurrection was the enthronement of Christ, <u>Acts 2:30, 31</u>. This is the simplest reality of *Acts,* out of which comes everything the apostles did and taught.

> *(David) was a prophet and knew that God had promised him on oath that he would place one of his descendants on his throne. Seeing what was ahead, (David) spoke of the resurrection of the Christ.*

In their natural thinking, the disciples didn't know it was going to happen like this. They thought in terms of what Judaism had said.

Jesus spent 40 days teaching them this, but even

after all that they still asked about a kingdom for Israel. Immediately upon expressing that thinking again, Jesus said to stop thinking about it, but that the Father was going to grant them the kingdom's power, through the arrival of the Spirit. The term *power* there is that of authorized representation and its effects or results. Someone needed to announce to both the mighty and the weak that the King was enthroned, and should be obeyed. They would be his envoys. So now they know something of the content, and channels and goals of the actual kingdom.

The end-result was going to be that many people from among the nations would believe and honor the Son as they should, including that they would in turn become *ambassadors* for the same King.

Did you hear correctly? The end-product of what was launched by Christ in the early chapters was a move to call even the greatest of your land or country to be an envoy for the sacrificial resurrected Christ! You will find that because of Psalm 2, this was how the apostles prayed, and at the end of Acts, in ch 26, they continue to pursue this. Their claim was aggressive; they did not just want to mention Christ, but to see the world's leaders perform double ambassadorship or at least assist the kingdom's envoys.

Any pursuit less than this allows the world to move into Marxism. But that point will be taken up at the end of this study.

Early *Acts* is grounded in the *enthronement* of Christ, the *appointing of envoys* who would declare that, and the *evangelism* of the world through them.

Infinite But Personal Power
It is very easy to fall into 2 traps about a manifestation of the power of God. One is to think he should do everything, perhaps everything *now*. This is why in general many people ask 'why didn't God do this or that?' Or 'what kind of God would let this happen?' It is a way of treating God as an impersonal force of goodness with infinite capacity.

People who have almost no regard for or acquaintance with the Bible seem to have an absolute knowledge of what God should do. Marxism fosters this, to ridicule God, a god only known through some dark experiences, who is blamed for not being an infinite force of *goodness*. Marxism expects the state to be that infinite force. Marxist atheism has no reasons for what it believes in the classic, direct sense. The fact that there is food and we have a system that can sustain us when we eat it is 'miracle' enough, if there was nothing else, to believe, as Paul told Greek philosophers in Acts 17. But Marxists do what they do, say what they say, to enable massive government.

Here in *Acts*, it leads to saying the events of *Acts* are not the kingdom of God at work because they fail to do *everything*: that the signs and wonders are limited; there are still opponents; Christians die as martyrs, etc.

But the things which happen, viewed in the positive light which they should be, show a steady, unstoppable, astonishing power. The tongues transmits the Gospel to all foreign languages of those attending Pentecost and going home. A healing may only be about one person, but it provides access to the leaders of the day. An arrogant monarch dies for thinking he is a god. The ground shakes as believers pray for all leaders to submit to Christ. A martyr sees the enthroned Christ *standing* in honor of him, just as plain as his persecutors saw him stand in front of them. 2 people die for defrauding Christ about a donation. Etc., etc. All of these exhibit astounding power but are not 'everything.' Because that is not the nature of the kingdom. Yet each of them is forceful in a meaningful way that can be told to others and that results in goodness. They are all limited but very intentional events.

Please bear in mind: I'm not writing this to say: here is how the Spirit works—or how God has the Spirit work—as though the material was instructing us for all time. I'm not resolving that you pray this way or that, or fast, or get away 40 days etc. I'm not trying to get you to see a millennium a certain way. I'm dealing with what happened *as a record* 'of the mighty acts of God' ch 2:11. I don't know if God is going to do any of this again. We simply want to understand that a 'startup' was executed, and see that it was successful, that it makes a public societal statement that God has planted something very worthwhile, and good, here on earth.

I Will Come the Way You Have Seen Me Depart
       After announcing they would have this role, he says he would come again just like his current departure. It was a quiet event. There was no fire out of heaven or overwhelming noises. The ground did not turn molten. He meant he could step back into their effort *at any time and do things*. They would do a lot, but he would also be there, and was. He meant that he was *that* near, that heaven was *that* near, and that he was about to do remarkable things. Sometimes he *would* appear again. The remark about coming, then, would be a confirmation of these things, and it was. Paul tells us in I Cor 15, that there were many times when he appeared.
       This was the 2nd item about early *Acts* that was 'stuck'--to me, and helped me see that something formidable was taking shape 'beneath' all the events. I simply had to dislodge it from being about the 2nd coming.

'I will come this way' is not about the 2nd coming which is an onslaught of destruction of an evil world. He was referring to the same thing as the later offer of 'sending Jesus' in 3:20, and that there would be further work by the Spirit, and the envoys and the same target-- the ends of the earth.

> *Repent... so that times of refreshing may come from the Lord, and that he may send the Christ...even Jesus. He must be received in heaven until the time comes for God to restore everything...*

We know that 3:20 is not an offer of another kind of thing (a restoration of Israel), because the next line after 'that he may send the Christ' is that *Christ is to remain honored* in his seat until the end of time. It is *another kind* of sending.

This was now the 3rd item in early *Acts* which had been 'locked' in a rather flat and stunted understanding. Three times now the plain meaning of a key verse simply did not go anywhere because I was not truly paying attention to it. Instead, I had paid too much attention to people invested in things they thought these lines were saying.

He would move seamlessly between heaven's cloud and earth, but in either case he would be establishing that he is to be honored by all for what he accomplished in the Gospel event.

I do not want the question of a millennium to block you from seeing what is going in *Acts*. That would be to totally miss how powerful it is. We are simply told that God is going to work, that it is his kingdom (because 'power' is a kingdom word-choice), and it is going to be like what he did before when he was on earth. The twin deadends of millennialism and its opposite both fail to plummet what is really going on. Neither are worth pursuing.

The passage is saying that Jesus would be 'sent' in a way that keeps him in his honored position throughout this age. How are both things done at the same time? Early *Acts* answers this: Jesus intervenes, usually through his envoys/witnesses, sometimes seen, and does things (or God does things on his behalf) *to be honored for all time.*

The Resurrection Is The Enthronement of the King
In Acts 2 we find that the resurrection is what David foresaw happening. It was not going to be a restored Judaic kingdom. It is what just took place--the resurrection of Christ, to which they were witnesses. As an indicator of his power, he gave the Spirit which launched the Christian message with overwhelming force. All those people had to do was return home talking about what they had seen, and the Gospel would go forward. God did this in a way to honor Christ throughout the world. *'Heaven must honor him.'* That is our 'map' of what

the Christian era would be like. More will be explained about the Spirit as a gift to the Son below.

The resurrection had been the seating of the Lord of no less than Ps 110. In that resurrection event, God made Jesus Lord and Christ. There is no pair of titles higher, though others will soon be added here in *Acts*. This being case, all of Israel was rattled at what to do next, which was to repent and *join the mission*, receiving the same gift of the Spirit. There are warnings that they needed to be saved from their generation, although maybe not with as much force as 3:23:

> '*Anyone who does not listen to the (prophet) will be completely cut off from among his people.*' (--Deut. 18).

The reason this forceful warning is there is that if Israel does not become missionaries, they will become hopeless revolutionaries. And most did. Those are the facts of the 1st century. You have to work out for yourself whether that meant the race-nation or the believers.

This kingdom continued. There was no overthrow of existing leaders, but there was a sign to which they were to respond favorably: a healing in ch 3. It is amazing how *much* can be done with just *one* healing miracle. God does not have to do 'everything' to make a considerable impact.

Instead, the leaders of Judaism tried to shut down the message of the resurrection, which undercut so much of their business. There is only one meaning of Ps 110 and the apostles had it. Given that meaning, yes, there was a decision whether to obey God rather than men. The difference between the Christian message and Judaism was now clear, 4:19, and attested (by the miracle).

The power of the kingdom now became a thing which the apostles consciously prayed about, 4:23+. That is, this new position Christ had was so tangible that all leaders and nations should be in subjection. They found themselves in the dilemma of Ps 2, which was originally a Davidic psalm question: *'why do the nations rage against the Lord and his Christ?'* So we now have two confirmations that what David was speaking of had come about; David's question would be asked as Christ's kingdom came. That is why in ch. 15, the Davidic platform (the raised fallen tent) of what is going on with nations coming to faith, is well established.

To be sure, the apostles also spoke of the resurrection in another sense: *proclaiming in Jesus the resurrection of the dead.* –Acts 4. Yet this is more related than you may think. Messiah is always shown to be a figure who pulled off a defeat of death. The others (the dead) which the apostles were speaking of here are those who believed in Christ and were raised in him.

The Appeal to Israel to Be Missionaries

The apostles knew the royal power of God had allowed the crucifixion and that it had allowed the event of Pentecost. It was Israel's turn to see that the message about the crucifixion (forgiveness for it) was Israel's task to take to the ends of the earth, instead of trying to shut that message down. Several thousand believed in the early days of the church, and that included many priests. The apostles envisioned the leaders even of Judaism and the pagan officials nearby to accept the position Christ now held, that Jesus is Lord, and Christ.

It should be clear that the apostles had a more aggressive objective than just getting fellow Israelites to believe. They wanted them to be *fellow mission workers.*

I would say that is probably the 4th item that kept begging to me to be understood, but did not really attach to anything until I realized the resurrection was the enthronement. It is not quite expressed in Acts 2's *'this message is for those who are near and for those who are far away'*, but it is certainly found in the end of 3's repeat that *'all the nations would be blessed through the Seed'* which is among the NT's top-quoted OT verse. Peter sees it as a destiny of Israel. This destiny figures again in Acts 13's tension with Jews, where Isaiah is saying that the group becomes the light to the world *through* entry into Christ.

Once again, we have to have a sense of what *Acts* is going to mean to Roman administrators when they heard

Paul's origins described. Paul (through Luke) was showing that the Christian faith was trying to get fellow Israelites *not* to revolt. They would still have some very challenging beliefs, but arming themselves to break up Roman control was not one of them. This is the subtext that comes through in *Acts*.

Nothing would have deflected the anger of Rome more than knowing that.

After that prayer in Acts 4, the place shook, and they continued to speak these same things boldly and full of grace. They 'continued to testify to the resurrection of Christ' meaning that *it was the enthronement* mentioned by David. It was never *merely* the fact of it happening, nor merely the fact that supernatural things could happen. It was the enthronement of Messiah.

The leaders of Judaism accepted supernatural things happening. They did not accept that they meant something against their beliefs, whether it was a healing or an enthronement claim.

Today, the 2nd coming fixation is so strong, people have no idea that Peter, who said 'God may send Jesus' for the mission, already knew that the 'sending' was about this mission, because of Jesus' 'coming as you have seen him go' of ch 1. But Jesus said he would come as they had seen him go: teaching, bestowing the power, reaching the nations, etc. These features are actually a set-up of Paul's role, even though in Acts 15, the apostles regarded Peter as 'sent to the Gentiles.' This was an odd thing to say—to point to *one* person--since Christ had made it clear, that his outreach would be to all nations.

So in addition to those new missionaries just created, the coming was referring to the interception of Paul for the mission of the Gospel to all the nations. We should say *'comings.'* Just remember the components:

1, teaching what the OT actually meant in Christ (this is why there is fundamental agreement between Paul and the apostles)
2, creating an envoy for the Gospel (Paul himself)
3, fulfilling the mission to the nation in all the prophets (as in the end of Acts 3).

Notice in Acts 15 in summary, that the apostles understood that Peter had been picked out to reach the nations, even though Paul would as well.

All of those things that the angels said were there 'as you have seen him leave, you will see him again.' It's not about the 2nd coming in judgement. There was no firey judgement when Jesus left the group right before Pentecost.

The Seating/Honoring of Christ
It is extremely important that we follow the connections made by Peter in the 1st 2 sermons/teachings. Why

suddenly talk about Ps 110? Because it was now fulfilled. But it obviously was not about a restored Judaic kingdom.

No, Ps 110 was referred to because the King had given out a gift for his own purposes which were successfully underway, no thanks to Judaism. That gift of the Spirit had in turn just been given *to him*! Remember, before his trial, Jesus had told Judaism that Psalm 110 wasn't about David's son in the normal sense; it was always about the Lord (the Son). And now he was seated/enthroned, as far as humans were concerned (it makes no difference to the Godhead).

As you will recall, this is where Judaism got stuck. They had no answer when he told them David's "son" was actually David's Lord. But this was no longer a surprise to the apostles because during the 40 days they learned that the resurrection had been foreseen by David, Acts 2:30, 31, *as the enthronement*.

The work of the Spirit here, the thousands who believed, and the healing of ch 3 are the official confirming signs mentioned in Heb 1-2, that Christ was enthroned exactly as Ps 110 meant (Heb 1:3, 8, 13) which is what David foresaw happening.

This is actual NT theology, as taught during the 40 day seminar.

If you really need a physical resemblance about the going and coming of Jesus of Acts 1 (rather than the list of 3 features I gave), then you need to show where the armies and firey blasts are happening in Acts 1 when he left. But they are not there. He must have meant something else. It is very important to see and preserve nuances of meaning.

Just as there is no connection between 'as you have seen him go up into heaven' in Acts 1 and the 2nd coming in judgement, there is also no connection between 'God will send Jesus' in Acts 3 (who must remain honored in his seat in heaven) and a restoration of Israel's kingdom as they knew it. It's just that in the early apostolic preaching and way of thinking, heaven was very, very close. It seeps through to earth in many events.

The fact that Acts 1-4 is full of kingship language is all I need to know to confirm that no "parenthesis" was in mind. The term power in Acts 1 is kingdom authority. That's it. That's what was planned all along, and is the fulfillment of all that the prophets had spoken, says the end of Acts 3. Subjection to the Son by the leaders of Judaism and the world leaders was prayed for in Acts 4 and the earth shook.

The Joy of Truth, and of 'Confirming' Suffering
Israel as a nation was given the opportunity to decide to be in that kingdom mission work. Most of them decided not to. That sets up the usual division between the race-nation and the remnant. Or the whole vs the true Israel, which is throughout the NT. The remnant is Gospel-believing Christians along with their Gentile counterparts.

26

The resurrection as the enthronement is such a strong force in the apostle's teaching in 1-4 that we now can understand the 'joy' of being detained for Christ.

You can recall that to witness/testify to the resurrection is not merely that a supernatural event took place. Because we don't find that kind of thing an issue in these settings. (Cp. 4:7 and 16; there is no undercutting of such events).

In 6:31 we hear Peter again saying that God exulted the Prince and Savior of Israel. The uproar that follows in Sanhedrin is not mere life from death, but *enthronement. The Prince is enthroned.* That's what they were witnesses of.

Another way to put it is: *Jesus was made the Christ.* Meaning the crucified, resurrected Jesus. It was not a reference to something X000 years in the future. Not a hint of that. The person who had just been killed, who was a sacrifice for sins, was the Christ which even Judaism was expected to see.

The meaning of the resurrection is what they proclaimed (4:2): that Christ was enthroned by that event, 2:30, 36. This was a notice to the whole nation, 2:36, because the whole nation was to become missionaries for the Gospel to all nations, 2:39.

So the 'corruption' in ch 2 and the 'wicked ways' in 3 were to be *in denial* of this package.

In 3:24, all the prophets spoke of these days, meaning, his enthronement, the signs, the Spirit, and the

27

decision that that generation of Israel had to make.

But there is still more besides Ps 2, 16 and 110 (which are the obvious 'top' ones to quote about such an epic event). We also see that Ps 118 is quoted, that the rejected cornerstone is now the capstone.

This is a Christocentric psalm; written well before he would actually be in the events where he would say them. They are the happy lines of Messiah being brought back from death and sin to save many people. That was the day the Lord had made for all to rejoice in. It also contains *'blessed is he who comes in the name of the Lord'* in other words, Messiah is coming back to his welcome procession at the right hand of God because his feat is accomplished, finished. The heavens roar with it (Acts 3:21 means to be seated in honor at a festival), although we got a small human taste of it a few days before the crucifixion, which the leaders of Judaism tried to shut down.

There is no confusion at all that it was time to exult in this psalm, which further infuriated the leaders of Judaism of Acts 4. But when a psalm says there will be rejection, and then there is the rejection, then there is a validation or *confirmation* of truth, which is the most rewarding experience in the world.

The psalm is not about an event X000 years in the future . Mt 23 uses it to pinch Israel with the reality that he gains that praise very soon in his victory. Those who sing it (the apostles in Acts 4) 'see him.' That's all it means. The

NT is unified, not a clatter of incompletenesses and fractures.

We can now understand something about the apostles' joy at being detained: *It's true! The enthronement is true!* There is nothing in the world that matters more to a person than gaining truth! They had now been taught it, they had seen signs and wonders due to it, they had received the very gift that the Father gave the Son upon his enthronement, and they had heard the powerful lines of Ps 2, 110, 118 from Christ and in their announcements to Israel.

So now, if the leaders of Judaism and the Gentiles attack them, it is the same power (royal permission, action, enactment, as in 4:28) that crucified Christ, and can only lead to honor of the same victory of Christ, even if they are jailed!

This shows how deep the honor of the enthroned Christ was meant to run. Whether out at the market or in jail, the believer had the truth about the world, but the unbeliever did not. That was everything that was needed! He could *do all things through Christ's strengthening.*

To be clear, it is not the physical blows themselves which the apostles enjoyed. They were not psychotics or masochists. It was that all that they had been taught was truth, *not fantasy, not fraud.* That means the enthronement in honor of Christ. Jailed or released; none of that mattered. Jesus had been sent and was at work. The age of Messiah and his mission was here; there was no going back; there was no undoing of it. Everything was set in place as had been announced beginning a couple years before.

My favorite paradox: the apostles are called 'unschooled'. Hey! There is no better school than the 40 day seminar of Acts 1:3.

No Conventional Kingdom

There really is not a trace of Judaism here in these unfolding events or the apostles' thinking about them. It is obvious that the apostles really missed the kingdom as far as its nature, in Acts 1, even after the 40 days training. I have been there. I have been through trainings and still not known what the real event trained for would be like.

But now we know what Christ meant about being with them or about them *seeing* Him. It was going to come in many interesting forms. *'Things never happen the same way twice.'* --Aslan

One of the simplest ways to understand the meaning of *Acts* is to ask: what is God doing, and what does He say he is doing? The 2nd is meant to draw attention to the OT quotes that 'explain' the present.

It is quite clear that there is no interest in a conventional 'kingdom of Israel.' Interest is dismissed up front, and in ch 26, we hear that Israel is missing what has taken place before their eyes. There is of course the kingdom of God, which is the kingdom of faith, of believers, in the Gospel, reinforced by sign after miracle, after powerful presentation, over and over. It is clearly meant to affect society: Acts 4 is a prayer against the rage of all leaders against the Lord and His Christ. All people on earth are to *'kiss (pay homage) to the Son.'* This message is taken to the ends of the earth.

There is a strategic reason for Paul why there is no mention of a conventional kingdom; the materials of Acts are to be read by Roman admins to decide if Paul is a zealot threat. Actually, to refer to a coming King David in their sense was sedition. The cynical inscription on Christ's cross "The King of the Jews" actually *helped* on this question about threat; that pathetic body was all the 'kingdom' there was. The power of the kingdom of God would come *another* way. Did it ever!

That's probably the most important thing this essay has to offer: for people to see that the kingdom of God is *his reign through the Spirit's powerful work* wherever the Gospel was preached.

The reference to the 'hope of Judaism' addressed in Acts 26 cements this. Israel was expecting one thing; Paul said it was already here. Just as at the beginning conflict in Acts 4, Judaism still has completely different expectations, despises hearing of the Enthroned King (and tries to leverage this as a danger to Rome, Acts 17:7) and persists in disagreement when Paul explains it.

The Resurrection Was the Enthronement

Let us now move on to ch 5 because of v31 regarding the Prince and Savior. That is 5 superlative titles for Jesus in 5 chapters. Obviously no other kingdom was intended.

There is no sense at all in Acts that there is an alternate plan going, a sidestep, a detour, an unforeseen problem, so that the mission to the nations is a surprise. Actually, the term power--the kingdom putting things into effect--is used to describe what God is doing in saving people as much as the crucifixion.

There were 5000 male believers in 4:4. In 6:7, even more, and "a large number of priests". (I wonder if this is where the Pharisee issue begins that results in ch 15's conference.)

How did Christ teach for 40 days and manage to say nothing clear enough about a supposed kingdom for Israel that the guys had to ask? Because he was teaching about the *actual* kingdom that was coming, or at least providing the OT background that needed to be taught in public.

How do the passages in Acts manage to say nothing of a conventional kingdom when they do touch on Israel? What was promised *has arrived in Christ and his resurrection.* That is the answer.

If you know the accusations against Paul in the end of Acts, you will be see the significance of the accusations against Stephen in ch 6: the leaders of Judaism claim he is speaking against Moses and God, against the holy place and the law, v 11+. There is even the detail that Jesus might destroy the place and change the customs. Well, I wonder how they got hint of that?

And so why doesn't this man full of the Spirit start teaching them about an ordinary kingdom for Israel right then, to stop the madness of persecution? *Couldn't Stephen have said something about a conventional kingdom? Instead we have the type of kingdom of God where the whole earth is a mere footstool for Messiah. This was because of the 40 days of teaching by Christ.*

If we do not understand the apostles and their fresh use of the OT, right off the 40 days of teaching, then we will think the Bible does not make sense--about its objective or Israel or the Gospel mission.

Exactly where these chapters say the mission to the nations, empowered directly by the Enthroned King, seen and unseen, is the total concern of the apostles--right there Judaism expected a repeated offer of a Judaic kingdom to Israel, with every intention of it being accepted.

Because of the 'great commission' and Lk 24's summary of Christ's post-resurrection talk, we should expect Acts to move forward essentially as it did. The idea that there is some change of objective is totally foreign,

Jesus Also Comes in Acts 23

Another instance where Jesus is sent to the apostles per Acts 1 and the reference to the mission is noteworthy. In the thick of conflict with mob-Judaizers in Jerusalem in Acts 23 is an appearance of Jesus to reinforce Paul.

What is noteworthy is the overall mission, which goes back to Lk 24--the commission. *'As you have testified about me in Jerusalem, so you must testify in Rome.'*

You will recall the early use of 'testifying' in Acts is to clarify that the resurrection was the enthronement David had in mind. It wasn't simply 'supernaturalism.' It was a shot across the mistaken bow of Judaism. We find this also in Paul's final letter, where we are to *remember the Gospel, Jesus Christ raised from the dead, descendant of David*, 2 Tim 2. The resurrection meant that he was that Son of David.

But now God or Christ is orchestrating an audience with the highest secular official of the time! Talk about establishing your presence! This is unstoppable. Not only will there be an audience with Caesar's court, there testimonial that Paul had insisted on his Roman civil rights will be recounted. It would be unmistakable that this tiny movement was being put forward to the greatest of the time just the same.

Connecting the resurrection and the Davidic line ticked off the Jews, obviously; but they in turn tried to get the Romans ticked off with the king/kingdom references.

But that would be to miss the point that it was not a kingdom of strength or power, but the Spirit. The Roman officials were not very good at dealing with that, but at least it was not the threat they imagined. Instead it was an appeal to the person's self-control and righteousness. A few years later, one emperor would try to make adultery illegal, but the effort failed.

The overall objective of the mission of Acts was to get the Gospel to all the earth, and to the kings of the world, and that meant Caesar. It did not fail.

The Gift *To* The Son
The gift that Peter mentioned was not Jesus' gift to the apostles. Again, we must step back from pet theories, and claims of experiences about how the Spirit did this or that. We must listen to the account. The account is about the enthronement of the Son, honoring him for his Gospel sacrifice. It was the Father's gift to the Son. The pouring out is the Father's gift *to the Son*. It is the Father saying: in honor of what the Son has done, I will pour out my Spirit so that all the ends of the earth may hear his fame and glory. The NT has several places where it shows this to be the plan of the Messianic age before it arrived. We have just heard the details above about speaking directly to Caesar.

This is what the passages say, but we are used to

thinking this is a gift *to us*. But it is only that as an *after effect* of the above.

I have no 'formulas' about the Spirit working, but I do have this observation about misplaced attention about the Spirit: *he was given to honor the Son.* Jn 14-17. He was not given for personal changes, though there will be. He was given to complete the understanding of the apostles, who, you may recall, were in the dark when they heard about the crucifixion and resurrection. He was also given to speak *about Christ* rather than himself. So any pursuit of how the Spirit works must be subject to whether we are pursuing the honor of Christ as enthroned King. If we are, the Spirit will work.

The Successful Honoring of the King

I hope I have cemented in your minds that the enthroned Christ of Acts 2:30, 31 is the frame of early Acts preaching and teaching. Our task is to enter into the Father's honoring of the Son, and to declare his glory as widely as possible.

From the Resurrection victory onward, there are nearly 2 months of sustained power among the disciples: the time of teaching, the announcement that they would be granted kingdom powers, the event of Pentecost, the healing, the powerful speeches of Peter, the increasing number of believers, the fellowship, the prayer that repeats what gains had been made in the granted kingdom power-

36

-that God would act again to 'outdo' the powers that be, so that they would know who was King and Enthroned. The ground quakes. Two people die for their pretension about devotion to the King. There is the powerful speech of Stephen ending with the vision that the Son of Man was standing up, not sitting, to receive him. Then there is the conversion of Paul with direct involvement of Christ. A king dies for claiming to be god; a relative of Peter is raised from the dead.

So there is quite a bit of 'seeing Jesus' or of God's *sending* him to act, as Peter had said, in ch 3. Enough to place the church solidly in history so that it cannot move. We don't know that these kinds of things are to continue happening, but that these things were meant to land the church. *'Blessed are those who have not seen, and yet believe'.* That line makes the historic records as powerful as the events themselves.

And then perhaps there is 'a quiet slipping away' (a Lewis' line about Aslan after the establishment of the kings and queens of Narnia). The arch-enemy of Christ is captured; more than that, he is turned into the leading proponent. This of course refers to Paul.

Things are now more or less settled and the church is powerfully planted and continues to grow and expand.

The picture painted is a success, a victory. God had indeed 'sent' Jesus as enthroned, through the founding and activity of his church. Humanly speaking, it should have failed.

Stopping the Tailspin of the Reformation-based West
I do not see where these principles from *Acts* are the regular food of churches these days, whose roots are the Reformation, where some of them were expressed.

As a spot-check of the impact, my research on the 'freedom of speech' trial of the *Crown vs Thomas Williams* in 1800 England revealed this fact as the trial of the revolutionary publisher was later summarized. You can find this in my 15 minute documentary BE CAREFUL WHAT YOU WISH FOR. The prosecutor Erskine actually began this trial of a revolutionary as a *blasphemy* trial. See how Christian doctrines were central to society? For all its faults, Erskine came to realize that Christian faith actually held the West together; England in particular.

Today the West is in a tailspin about its identity as it drifts further and further the roots of *Acts*. To affirm the resurrection as a miracle is not quite the force that the NT has; our society needs to hear this. To believe in one way for the Spirit to work, based on this or that line from early *Acts* is not really what it was trying to say. To tangle about supposed references to a millennium or a future for Israel also badly misses what is going on, and weakens the power of the picture.

The Christian believers should be unified in telling their state leaders that those leaders have their positions through the enthroned Christ who is to be honored. This is apostolic thinking. It is not that Christians are trying to *become* the state, but trying to get the state to subject itself to a universe in which Christ is enthroned in honor. This is a standard part of Paul's theology (Col 1:16), but I do not recall hearing it taught by any Christian pastor or teacher in the past decade, nor on radio (sampling 1-2 hours a day).

The apostles were *that* aggressive in their stance toward the powers that be. They taught obedience to the state generally, but also taught things that put Rome in its place in *Christ's* universe. (Disputes with Judaism's leaders are in a slightly different category). *"The obedience of Christians to the state should be obvious, so that when they need to express dissent, it will be heard"* —Udo Middelmann in PRO-EXISTENCE.

The impact of the early church on souls (and structures after that) cannot be missed. I don't know how we can not see the turbulence among pagan institutions in *Acts* when the Gospel is around. Nor see that the kingdom would come and be *"the rock that struck the statue (and) became a huge mountain and filled the whole earth."* Daniel 2.

If the church's teachers miss these basics—as Marxist historians and transformationalists would like them to--is it any wonder that society in general acts out on such poorly kept information? We are seeing this all over the streets of the West today.

It should be clear to all from this year's events that Marxism has no real structure at its end; it is chaos. More to the point: it is *suicide*. Don't kid yourself that it has another 'structure' in mind. Structure has to do with Christ, and it abhors Christ. There are no 'mission statements' it can make now that can be trusted. This is intentional. It knows that real structure derives from the enthroned Christ to spread his honor. It knows of NT passages such as 1 Timothy 2 where prayer for kings and leaders is commanded so that the world hears of the enthroned Christ *again*.

The Christ who was violently humiliated by Rome was back, in Caesar's court, unstoppable, telling him that the reason Caesar existed was to honor Christ! Show where in early *Acts* the Davidic vision was something other than what the apostles accomplished. You cannot. We are to find and pursue the channels for this same effect in our generation.

Is there any chance the name of the Marxist 'country' created in Seattle used the term 'autonomous' which Dr. Schaeffer used as the opposition to the Lordship of Christ?

The reason the Marxists want you confused about the enthronement, or the Spirit, or the mere supernatural-ness of the resurrection is to divide and conquer the West.

There's no place for an enthroned Christ, Lord of the universe, in Marxism.

Confusion contributed by churches may perhaps just be due to a slight language distortion which was popular in the 70s. It *individualized* something that was *cosmic*. The teaching of Christian faith in the 70s would say that '*you the individual* needed to make Christ Lord of *your life*.' If you say this 1000x and *don't* say that Christ is the enthroned King of the universe that David saw, a different picture will appear, and it will not be the powerful objective NT picture.

2

The Davidic References of Early Acts

Odd as it may seem, David is mentioned a lot by the apostles. That is, his kingdom is:

"God had promised him...a descendant on his throne. ...he spoke of the resurrection..."

"David didn't ascend to heaven, yet he said, 'The Lord said to my Lord ('be enthroned')...'"

*"Christ is

*'the stone you builders rejected, which has become the
capstone.'"* –Psalm 118, by David

*"You spoke through our father David:
'Why do the nations rage...against the Lord and...Christ.?"*

*"What God promised our fathers he has fulfilled...by raising up
Jesus...says the 2nd Psalm:
'You are my Son'*

*"The fact that God raised him from the dead...is stated in these
words:
'I will give you the holy and sure blessings promised to David'*

*"for when David served God's purpose in his own generation, he
fell asleep. But the one whom God raised from the dead did not
see decay..."*

*"Simon has described how God at first showed his concern by
taking from the Gentiles a people for himself. The words of the
prophets agree:
'After this I will return and rebuild David's fallen tent.'"*

It is simply a matter of realizing that the kingdom being
spoken of was what was said to be delivered in the event
of the Spirit at Pentecost. 'You shall receive power' is about

a kingdom that was so unstoppable, it put Paul smack in front of Caesar's court, to tell him that he was to honor Christ. But that was an aside accomplishment. It's first was to declare Christ as God's gift of redemption to the nations.

The final time that the Judaism of the apostles surfaced (Are you restoring the kingdom now?), the above was the answer: 'you will receive kingdom power,' making their question the wrong question.

The Davidic kingdom theme in Acts

We already know that in Acts' first page and last full-length speech, the Christian faith has no interest in or pursuit of a restored kingdom of Israel. 'We do not teach beyond what the prophets have said--the sacrifice of Christ and him being preached to the nations.'

What we may not notice is the connection between this and the Davidic kingdom theme, stating things in the positive, but not what Judaism wanted.

1, the King is enthroned in the resurrection. This was foreseen by David (who is called a prophet there) in Acts 2. This is the triumphant climax of Acts 2--God has made Jesus Lord and Christ. There is no theory about this; in Acts 4 during the outbreak of conflict, the apostles prayed that the kings of the earth and the rulers of peoples would stop their opposition to the Lord and Christ. This is called 'the apostles doctrine' which means that we have clarification of what was taught in the 40 day seminar, and have heard it preached once.

2, the resurrection was the transfer of the promises/blessings for David to Christ, Acts 13, quoting Ps 2, Is55 and Ps 16. It is quite clear that what was expected for David no longer exists as such and has found its expression in Christ. It is the thing which the prophets said:

'I am going to do something in your day which you will not believe even if someone told you.'
--which is Acts 13 from Hab 1.

Obviously the apostles' taught that what had taken place in Christ is where this found fulfillment. Not the future.

Yesterday I was listening to the KJV being read on 13:42 and it said that the *Gentiles* asked Paul to teach further, meaning the ones who attended synagogue. The whole city came! This is because the blessings promised to David had been unlocked and opened to all who believe; it was justification from sins.

Whatever other purpose God had in David 'was served in his own generation.'

The Jews mostly were too saturated with the 'unworthiness' that the Law projects and details, and would not accept such a great piece of news.

3, the amount of non-Jews who believed would soon be called the 'raised fallen tent of David' in Acts 15. I'm not sure where from, but the idea of a lowly 'tent' that would include all nations is back there, and had been dropped (mentally) with all the glamour of an actual temple. Perhaps it is simply connecting the humility of David and Christ.

These things have been known for ages, v18; there is no mystery about it.

The mistakes on these things by Dispensationalism are so many, this article would have to be 3 times larger to explain.

As a reminder, *Acts* begins and ends by saying that some kind of restored kingdom for Israel as they knew it was not to be explored. Nor does it ever surface. The whole force of what Paul says in Acts 26 is that what has taken place in his life-work, in the Christian faith, was what the prophets said would come. He said this in light of the fact that his countrymen in Jerusalem, 'serve God day and night, hoping to see the promise fulfilled.' He then jumps to the fact of the resurrection. But that is not to change topics. It is because it is the topic that matters; Christ is enthroned 'as David foresaw' and in a way that transfers the blessing to Christ.

Now comes an important warning for handling all this: if you do not treat the Bible as unified on one kingdom, if "David's kingdom" is miles away from "Daniel 2's" etc, *over and over,* you will just divide the coherence of the Bible up until it is meaningless. In Eph.1, the title Christ gained is above every title *in this age and the next.* We hardly need to look for anything else that ties it all together.

3

The 40 Days
and The Earliest NT Quotes of the OT

The Initial Dejection of the Disciples

It is very important to realize that the gospel narratives are trying to capture a developing sequence for us. We find this introduced, for ex., in Jn 2 about destroying the temple. A concept is introduced (a new temple), but they didn't understand *until after* the resurrection what Christ meant. The statement is obviously highlighting the time lapse between Jesus expressing it, and the followers understanding it, a couple years later. Guess when the 40 days of teaching the disciples "all over again" took place?

The disciples were dejected about the death of Christ because of lingering doctrines of Judaism. They had thought Jesus was going to 'redeem' Israel. It is not difficult to find people thinking the same thing when Christ was born in early Luke's nativity narratives.

But please understand why Luke would do so. He was providing material to show that Paul was *not* part of any violent revolutionary group because the featured 'redeemer' did not go down that path, and indeed, he attempted to convert zealots. The hesitation of people about Jesus' including Galileans was that they were from a hotbed for revolution. Chapter 6 of this book will integrate that kind of information about 1st century Judea.

So it is not complicated to realize that the disciples were dejected at his death. It is not easy to absorb a concept based on a dead person coming back to life! But then there is an additional fork in the road: would that resurrected person *now* supernaturally overthrow Rome and cause the vivid Isaianic visions to take place? After all, that resurrection was quite a demonstration of an unusual power!

The answer of early Acts (and where else would we find it but in the preaching of early Acts?) is that it is neither X000 years in the future in a revisit of what ancient Israel was like, nor is it a danger to Rome. But it is the occupied throne of David, and the whole universe is to take note, and honor the Son.

It is the explanation of this which takes place in the 40 days, and is summarized as 'explaining the kingdom of God.' The next and only place we can look after that is the earliest uses of OT quotes. There is no other place but Acts to look. Here is a quick list of OT quotes that are the earliest known. Some of them are quoted again in the earliest letters. The object is to identify what was being *taught in the 40 days, summarized as Christ suffering and being preached among the nations,* in Lk 24. It says that fulfilled all that was written in Moses and the Prophets.

One of the interesting features I noticed was that the quoting was broad-based; you will not see many repeats; many passages were drawn upon to make the same conclusion as the others. That is encouraging to know the NT is unified that way.

If Hebrews is as early as the 40s, then the frequency of repeating certainly changes. But the breadth remains.

Our theology should resemble and echo what the apostles emphasized, to be *Biblical,* that is. If you are just referencing a few of these to build and protect a 'system' don't bother calling it Biblical theology.

Early NT fulfillment quotes continuity worksheet

The study assumes we don't have a written NT *letter* until the late 40s, @ Acts 15. The assumed gospels order of completion is Mark, Matthew, Luke, John.

Joel 2: 28-32   Acts 2

The theme here is that we are in the last days of signs and wonders and visions, and when the outreach to the nations would be completed as simple as 'call on the name of the Lord.' Rom 10 adds that they can't call unless there are missionaries, which appeal had been made to Israel over and over (not a government kingdom) and then to Gentiles.

Ps 16:8-11   Acts 13

Like Acts 2 the official interp of Ps 16 is that the person in the Psalm is Christ, and the return to the right hand of God in other psalms is the same as being taken to his presence of this one.

These uses are not simply saying 'the OT is talking about the resurrection.' They are saying the resurrection is the enthronement. David has come and gone, but his seed was Christ and what was meant to be accomplished is found in the resurrection. The reason it was accomplished was for the mission to the nations.

Ps 110:1   Acts 2

The resurrection is the enthronement of Christ. This is
what David foresaw, and the participial adverbs (to have
the role of prophet and to know) are setting up *David spoke
of the resurrection.* He was not speaking of a supposed
millenium at all, because the supporting verses here are
regarding the resurrection (Ps 16, the placing of a seed on
the throne) and neither David's work in his life nor his
ascending above was meant. Acts 13 also says this kind of
thing about David in that 'the purpose of God in his time
was completed.'

Compare Mk12: the exchange about Ps 110. The upshot of
this exchange is distance from David in the usual sense. It
was the Lord who was honored with the enthronement.
The Acts 2 passage says this enthronement is now *past
tense*; has taken place; God *has made* Jesus Lord...

Gen 22:18   Acts 3:25

This and the next are the famous Seed passages. In the
Seed of Abraham, all the nations of the world would be
blessed. The Seed, says Paul, is one person, not many
people, unless you mean people "in the Seed." But the
blessed are many people.

The reason we find this mentioned and Paul saying the

same thing is because there is one gospel shared by Peter and Paul.

If you think 'these days' in 3:24 is a leap to X000 years in the future, you are forgetting that Peter just warned Israel sharply in the previous line. He was not absorbed in events X000 years in the future. The normal sense of reading these things is about *that* moment, *that* decision, *that* generation, *their* 'wicked ways'.

It is further proof that there is no mystery that any of this would happen, only how--the channel of Christ, the Gospel.

Gen 26:4
See above about the Seed.

Ps 118:22   Acts 4
The Cornerstone psalm is quoted because Christ founded the kingdom and is the person about which people must decide. They may stumble on him; they don't need to. But he will also one day crush those on whom He falls.

Ps 2:1, 2   Acts 4
This psalm is about the day the Son is declared to the world, which He created and over which He is the true Lord. The expression 'you are my Son' is used at the

baptism of Christ followed with 'in whom I am well-pleased.' It was almost the beginning of Christ's ministry. It was heard again at the Transfiguration, when the clouds of heaven enveloped Christ, Moses and Elijah.

(I won't be using the examples of Acts 7 here as it is only a retelling of Israel's history, not direct declarations about Christ.

Is 53:7, 8   Acts 8
The question of who is Isaiah 53 about to be answered in the exchange.

Ps. 2:7   Acts 13
Once again we have: the resurrection is the enthronement. The Psalm quoted is the enthronement 'you are my Son' but the introduction by Paul is that it was the resurrection event.

('Raised up' in 13:33 is not the general profile-raising of Jesus ministry. That's above in 26+. This is the resurrection.)

This event fulfills 'the promise' to the fathers. Most of Israel knew the land was fulfilled in Joshua. But there was more to come. Not the land again, but the things that come through the Spirit--a real obedient people, a mission to the nations.

Is 55:3   Acts 13:34
God's raising Jesus from the dead was the transfer of the blessings from David to Christ. This is an echo of the fact that the resurrection is also the completion of promises to Israel. This is what David foresaw (2:31), but Peter did not mention the proof of Is 55:3 when he said that.

Hab 1:5   Acts 13
Habbakkuk's warning is repeated toward the Jews to respond to the Gospel. Resurrecting Christ as the fulfillment of their promises was the 'thing that was done in their time which they would not believe when told.'

Is 49:6   Acts 13:47
This passage from Isaiah was picked because it is probably clearest that the restoration of Israel (in the 4th century BC) was a much smaller goal than what the next age of Messiah would accomplish. But it is not the part Paul quoted. What he quoted was the part about it being a light to the nations.

he says:
"It is too small a thing for you to be my servant
to restore the tribes of Jacob
and bring back those of Israel I have kept.

I will also make you a light for the Gentiles,
that my salvation may reach to the ends of the earth."

This is spoken to the servant, and that is Christ. God made Christ a light for the Gentiles (which Paul quotes again in ch 26) but those who believe in Christ become that light as they lift Christ up.

<u>Amos 9:11, 12</u>   <u>Acts 15</u>
This passage is officially interpreted by James.
The return: after the captivity, Messiah comes and accomplishes redemptive things.
David's fallen tent raised: this is the ongoing faith-based believers, not the race-nation. The 'rebuilding' of the temple was first mentioned by Christ in <u>Jn 2</u>.
the remnant of mankind: like the original temple dedication song (<u>I Chron 16</u>), the nations come in through this rebuilt temple. The NT quotes that song many times.
the Lord does these things: indeed!
that have been known for ages: The first promise of the Gospel is in <u>Gen 3</u>. <u>Gal 3</u> says <u>Gen 12</u> preached the Gospel in advance, and Abraham believed, that justification would be granted by believing on the gift of the Seed, which would in turn bless all nations.

James says Peter knew God was seeking Gentile believers, so 'at first' means right away as the church started in

Pentecost. He didn't mean the Genesis passages, although it is there.

Romans Holds the Record for Quotes Per Chapter

Of course, once you move away from the earliest, freshest quotes, you must go to Romans to see a massive number of quotes (in the 70s). Even if you remove the dense collection about the sinfulness of man in ch. 3, you still are far above other letters, the 2nd place award going to Galatians 3.

The social situation of Romans may explain this. Jews were returning to Rome from the Claudian banishment. They were surprised at how well Gentile believers could have done on their own, and ch. 14 especially shows some strain between them. To help bond the two groups back together, Paul showed what he meant with many scoops of OT passages.

Every believer, not to mention every pastor, should have their own file of Romans quotes of the OT. The NIV footnotes these.

4

The Top 5 Accomplishments of the Kingdom,

in *Acts*, 'Humanly Speaking'
Answering those who think there is no visible trace of a kingdom, or it is a mess, or it is a failure

If you were to think in terms of the most impacting accomplishments of the apostles, in Acts, I think you would probably have a list something like this:

1, a sudden launch of Christian fellowship that is mission-oriented. Within weeks there were 5000 men.
At the same time, the people who returned home from Pentecost were 'automatically' accomplishing missions because they had to explain the relation between the curious event they attended and the previous events of Christ.

2, interception of the arch-enemy Paul
"Always know the counter-arguments" is the best rule when you are trying to put forward a new idea. So God seized the leading *counter-arguer* and by the time He was done, He had the church's main spokesperson. The new faith was now defended by the person who had sought to destroy it. His arguments against how Judaism saw things are the most vital.

3, presentation at the central exchange of Greek philosophy, the Aeropagus, Athens. This was a key event in meeting the darkness of unbelief, even if had slightly cracked the door open to faith (the unknown god). It is curious that archeology has recovered no churches in the area, though certainly around most of Greece. Or they simply did not use buildings of their own. There is also an important 'initiator' feature to notice in Athens. Paul talked to people in the market until a member of the Aeropagus invited him. Bingo. That's the best way in.

4, causing the collapse of 1.5 pagan cults in Little Asia. These accounts are in Ephesus, Acts 19, where because of an act of driving out an evil spirit, a whole network of astrology collapses. This is followed by the public humiliation of the Artemis cult.

This should not be separated from the fact that Paul worked out of a lecture hall for 2 years after this so that 'everyone in the province heard the word of the Lord.'

5, ongoing proclamation about Christ as King to Caesar, a 2 year residence in the palace. Writing Philippians from Rome, Paul shows that even chained, he has had a sustained effect on the palace (possibly palace guard) of Caesar. It is a curious picture: he's confined, but his speaking is not. I would think *that* would have been the 'dangerous' part.

While these things were the major signs of the kingdom of God at work, the destruction of Israel was coming into view. This event has an certain inevitability to it; the only direction Israel could go was toward a destructive revolt if it did not go to work in the mission of the Gospel. This will be the topic of ch. 6, Integrating NT History.

If you do not see the 'power of the kingdom' in these outcomes, along with all the more individual instances that took place through *Acts*, I don't know what else can show it. They were not meant to be 'everything.' They were meant to be the pattern, and some of them have been repeated elsewhere.

5

The Reign of Christ
In the Reformation Sense

from the Magdeburg Confession to the Dominion Voting Machines

I'd like to explain something that should matter to all of us interested in theology because we just passed the 500th anniversary of the first action of the Reformation--Luther's list of theses. All Western believers are related to this event. All Protestant sub-groups in conflict with each other, are in conflict with each other because of misunderstanding what it established.

The Reformation, as Dr. MacPherson of Bethany Lutheran College shows, is very important to the US Constitution because of the Magdeburg Confession, which was an initial statement of constitutional questions for Germany.

I don't know of another set of organized research and thinking that swept the West like it since the beginning, although Luther was guided by certain thoughts in Augustine. I'm referring to the cultural as well as theological sweep. The Reformation put a high value on this world and its features compared to its setting. In artistry and culture it was humanist, but not in its moral stance.

Here are some of the basics:

1, the Reformation said that it was **imputed grace** in Christ, not infused grace in our lives, that was meant by justification. This was not meant to be taken advantage of, but some did and became licentious. It does not deny changes in people. But it certainly shifted the attention away from the limits of things that can happen in our lives to the reality of what took place in Christ outside of us. Christ's righteousness was called 'an alien righteousness' by Luther, to get across that it is not in us. Imputation has to do with accounts, with sin as debt, with credit, and the believer is regarded by God *as if* he had the righteousness of Christ.

1A, the Reformation taught that there was a legal and personal part of salvation: justification, and then transformation or moral salvation. Justification has to do with **sin as debt**, so the NT terms are credit, reckon, impute, transfer, account, etc. Even *reconcile* in 2 Cor 5 should be thought of in bookkeeping terms first, not some mushy category (a 1970s life of Christ translated it 'God is now friends with the world.'???) Justification causes a great deal of personal change, but it is *not* the personal change itself.

2, the Reformation was **historically realistic**. In the following century, the understanding of the warning of the 'little apocalypse' of Jesus in Mk 13 etc was so clear that it inspired striking paintings about the destruction of Jerusalem. The most familiar is a huge piece that organizes the 3 synoptics and Paul in their warnings to the city about what would take place. Each of the writers is shown being guided by an angel.

The artists Durer and Rembrandt produced a number of highly realistic renderings of Biblical scenes which was unusual for the time.

Music also elevated, and as recently as this year, I attended a classics concert in which the hostess/cello player lamented at the end that things were a bit dark in all the modern compositions, so to lighten up, we would be taken back to a Bach for *inspiration*. It was one of his pieces for Lutheran worship. With the threat of the Black Plague, the Little Ice Age, and Islamic armies, the world of the Reformation had more to be angry about than we do, yet it was more inspired, and happier. With an enthroned King, there was less victimization.

The enthroned King theme produced this soaring piece of music by Charles Wesley:

Rejoice the Lord is King: Your Lord and King adore!
Rejoice, give thanks, and sing, and triumph evermore:
Lift up your heart, lift up your voice!
Rejoice, again I say, rejoice!

Jesus the Savior reigns, The God of truth and love;
When He had purged our stains He took His seat above...

His kingdom cannot fail, He rules over earth and heaven;
The keys of death and hell are to our Jesus given...

Rejoice in glorious hope! Our Lord the Judge shall come,
And take his servants up to their eternal home...

3, in **the science of interpreting**, the Reformation had some principles upon which many people faulter by departure from them. The most important were the set on how parts or types of material should be used to interpret others:

First, the NT interprets the OT. No brainer. There are some 2500 usages. But it is remarkable how many times this is by-passed or considered last!

Second, the *letters* interpret the gospel and narrative accounts. That insures that an isolated incident does not have the weight of a declaration.

Third, the ordinary-language *doctrinal* chapters interpret the symbolic.

Fourth, the complete or *systematic* treatments interpret the singular or exceptional references.

4, the Reformation was grounded in **science** with the work of the German geologist Steno and others. He organized the geologic record into the stages seen in Genesis: creation, the world before and after the deluge and the final state now. This was worked out in the 1700s and the basic outline was pirated a hundred years later to try to accommodate the massive time periods that uniformitarian atheism needed to make sense. In Luther's time, the science of language was in renaissance.

5, there was **another kind of "Israel"** according to the Reformation that was now at work to 'take the land.' Ie, to declare the authority of the enthroned Christ to the nations. It was found in Rom 9 and Eph 2-3, etc. This also shows in several hymns about 'marching to Zion' and other borrows of Israel-imagery. One of Luther's tracts was 'The Babylonian Captivity of the Church' which was written while he was still thinking there was a way for the institution to be whole, for him to remain in it. But obviously he borrowed on Israel's history. This could lead to anti-semitism, but not necessarily.

As one documentary on the life of Luther has shown, he had the same attitude as Rom. 11's 'prodding' of Israel to be evangelists for most of his work. When a daughter died under the care of a Jewish doctor (if you were 'anti-Semitic' you probably would *not* have a Jewish doctor), he was upset with Jews in his grief. He was in pretty poor health when he wrote that treatise.

6, there was an overall sense that **Biblical material was complete, coherent, and inspiring,** and forceful in its impact on the world. It made sense of things and was not treated as though it was 'religious truth' having a separate set of criterion. The idea of Darby and Scofield that *the Bible did not make sense* would have been utterly foreign to most people operating in the Reformation framework. I mention this because of the fact that 'Dispensationalism' which those two started, and has always said there are two programs that don't reconcile in the Bible. The Bible is thus hopelessly split without extensive explanation by them. You will find that the interpretive guides of the Reformation (feature #3) were also ignored by Dispensationalism, and that eventually the Dispensationalist movement was as much about infused grace (#1) as any other.

7, **politically and economically**, the Reformation gave groups the courage to form and define constitutions on their own, apart from the Papacy. This gave birth to independent nations apart from the Holy Roman Empire. Sometimes it was risky, like the Augsburg Confession and its awareness of having to face Islam without the help of the HRE. Sometimes it was abused, of course, like Henry the 8th forming a separate church simply because the Pope would not permit a divorce of the Spanish wife Kathryn. People sought the free market and venture capital to accomplish plans that created more wealth and work. The credited righteousness of Christ was a model for venture capital.

The Magdeburg Confession came as the second generation of Lutheranism started. The city had broken with the papacy about money before Luther, and had survived a 400 day siege by the HRE army. As Dr. MacPherson explains, there were 4 levels of political resistance:

Level 1: The Governor Who Was "Not Excessively Atrocious"
Level 2: The Lawless Tyrant
Level 3: The Coercive Tyrant
Level 4: The Persecutor of God
--*The Magdeburg Interpretation of Romans 13: A Lutheran Justification for Political Resistance,* July, 2016

As you can see, the list overall takes a dim view of office *holders*, unlike the euphoric and wishful view of politicians today. Abuses of level 2 were where *interposition* by magistrates should protect the citizen victim. At level 3, there should be a recall, a removal procedure. In cases of level 4, the Confession believed the tyrant should sentenced to death.

In all cases, the Lutheran understanding was that the office of those who kept order in the state (Rom. 13) was constitutionally defined, as well as divinely based. An *office holder* who failed to do so, or operated outside the definition, was to be dismissed. This system in itself cleared up many miserable and corrupt political situations.

The distinction between office and holder reached Calvin and Knox, and Knox's Geneva Bible (English) began to be imported to England, spreading awareness there.

There was a good intention among some of the Dispensationalists that was meant to clear up conflict in the English world between Protestants and Catholics. The Reformation nearly always referred to the Pope as antichrist. One list I've seen shows about 20 better-known Reformation preachers in agreement on this. The Plymouth Brethren hoped to defuse this problem in their country by saying the AC was a future figure, not the Pope. From what I know of sectarian strife and violence, I can't blame them for trying something.

What did Luther say was the 'standing or falling doctrine' of the church? It was that Christ's righteousness was imputed, not infused. The believer's blessing in Christ rather than the limited blessings in his own life, were his bright hope and anchor. If that was lost, everything was darkness. A modern God-Is-Dead theologian was once quoted saying *'God is a little voice in your head that says you're not good enough.'* Exactly; that's *dead* alright. The Gospel of the Reformation was the *ever-living* Christ of history (not in your head) with justifying righteousness for 'the least of these,' so that in Christ alone they are good enough.

The Meaning of the Dominion Voting Machine Scandal
Joseph Biden said in campaign footage that the voting machine scandal would be the greatest act of voting fraud in the history of America. He also said that to rule by executive order is a dictatorship. He is guilty of both and his remaining in position is destructive to the dual divinity-humanity of the US Constitution. The divinity, of course, is in locating the basis of rights in God—*above* the state. The humanity is that this check must check *with the people*, so as to not 'belong' to *too small* of a group of the citizens. Notice how Marxism cannot conceive of the basic ingredient of the divinity, and always tends to abuse the expression 'by the people.' Marxism's atheism is irrational of course, but extremely useful to a massive state.

The failure to correct the voting machine scandal will mean the end of Constitutional liberty.

The Lindell report ABSOLUTE PROOF has come out, solidifying the analysis of the election fraud claims. At one point on Fri.Feb.5, the Twitter trending for it was about 90,000.

I do not know where any optimism can spring from this, because none of the officials who participated in this mass crime have seen any consequences. In the late minutes of the documentary, two very high officials lament that the law enforcement organizations established to protect the US from such attacks (cyber attacks by other countries) are doing nothing. I'm not sure if Lindell's vision of a 'great revival' includes great *enforcement* and *incarceration*; hundreds were involved and have broken the one 'sacred' thing left about the American system.

At the same time, the Democrat party is pushing H.R. 1 through as quickly as possible. This bill formalizes all the things just done in the 2020 election, to make sure they are the standard procedure going forward. There will be no more fair elections.

The Reformation basis of our liberties will be gone because Marxism wants its massive state, and the history of the West is in the way. They have a man getting rid of it by Executive Order.

To bludgeon what our history actually means, the Left is running its 1619 Project, saying that the West exists for white racists.

Why People Left Europe For America, c. 1600-1800
The Left's other weapon against the Constitution is racism. The 1984-style rewrite of this is the 1619 Project, supposedly dating the start of the racist taking of the West.

Here is a recent example of re-writing history. I visited Pendleton, OR, and sure enough the rodeo stadium dominates certain views from the main street of the old town. It is known far and wide. It's on ESPN. What you may not know, and I did not, is that Happy Canyon is right next door.

Happy Canyon is an amphitheater on which an annual re-enactment week is held. The 4 confederated local tribes and the cowboys re-enact the original meetings and rendezvous of the Oregon Trail families and the natives. There's no disease outbreak, no fights, no massacres. They exchange and trade and compare music, etc. Far fewer people know of this annual re-enactment. It's easy for history to be re-written or written-out, or -off.

Among other flaws in the 1619 project, here are some counter-arguments which help us understand why people came to the West.

First, there was little expectation finding much of anything out there, let alone *anyone*. They expected to reach Asia. Once they learned there were people there, and it was not Asia, there was no predisposition to inflict *anything*. The new arrivals simply hoped there was a place available, free of the past problems.

Second, people wanted to leave Europe because of the degree to which Islam had taken several European countries.

Shakespeare mentions half of Italy in one his pieces. Vienna was nearly taken in 1683. In Moldova, in 1515, Stepan, helped by the King of Poland, diverted some of Islam's armies and *qom* (entourage) south and north. One burst of progress for Lutheran independence was due to the Holy Roman Empire's entanglements with Islam; there simply weren't enough resources to deal with Germany at the same time. Alternately, the Treaty of Crepy was a declaration by an Islamic general to *leave* the European theater for 5 years and attack. As my novel MANSFELDER FREIHEIT! shows, this is when Germany lost some of its pluralism and liberty; it was restored when the Lutherans worked out the Magdeburg Confession.

An additional reason for leaving Europe was the sectarian conflicts. This affects the American features of independence much more than the conflict with Islam. We wrote an article that prohibits state churches.

A third reason was the Little Ice Age, 1650—1875. Crop destruction and sickness led many to start over somewhere warmer.

Some British merchants took up the Islamic practice of slave-trading Africans. The numbers that were taken to America were well below those taken to Brazil, and those which Islam took to Arabia suffered badly from dysentery, and this is true even in present times.

In more modern times, millions left Europe because of Marxism-Leninism, but the 1619 Project will never tell you that white people in those countries were made 'slaves'—the ones who couldn't escape. "The average young person today is far more concerned about George Floyd than about the millions killed by Lenin." --Dennis Prager.

With the documentation in ABSOLUTE PROOF, we see the machinery of the loss of Reformation freedoms—the Dominion Voting Machine. If Prager is right, that 'the Left is the fastest growing religion in the West,' then we are back to Magdeburg.

The bitter, negative view of the West in Marxism works back from the machines (a violation of the sacredness of voting) to Engel's celebration of the German Peasant Revolts (on which Luther called down the sword of civil authorities) and back to the mob of the French Revolution and back to zealot revolt of 1st century Judaism.

I hope that you have seen the Reformation view of Christ's reign: all things improve when under his title as King. The resurrection has placed him above every title that can be named. In the next chapter, we will see the unmistakable consequences of failing to submit to the Son—the ravages of revolution.

No state church is envisioned by this teaching. However, if 80 million Americans were to tell their representatives the roots of liberty in the Reformation West, and individually vote and act this way, we might save the West.

6

Integrated New Testament History

A Basic History of 1ˢᵗ Century Judea Through The Masada Event in 72

One theological force which reduced the power of the humanism and revolution in the19th century was a presentation by Pastor George Holford on the destruction of Jerusalem of 66—72 AD. His interest was to restore the place of the divinity of Christ after all the attacks of Paine and of the reduction of Christ to his morals and ethics (and nothing else) by Jefferson's New Testament. Holford traveled all around England.

But Holford was heard by a London legal team often representing revolutionaries, and the team was shocked. They realized they were acting to destroy society and civilization. When Erskine and Kyd declared that the facts and doctrines about the destruction of Jerusalem undeniably reinforced the basic claims of Christianity — even if there were nothing else (and there was) — England listened, at least for a while. This development is found in my documentary BE CAREFUL WHAT YOU WISH FOR at Youtube.

But then the rest of the 19th century came along, and three destructive forces were at work which pertain to this book: Marxism, evolution and Dispensationalism. We do not need to spend time on evolution here. It is a fraud that is thoroughly treated. As the multi-honored research Dr. Wilder-Smith says in one of his titles, "Biology knows nothing of evolution."

Astonishing Similarities
But unfortunately we must take up the operational similarities of Marxism and Dispensationalism, which will trouble many readers. I acknowledge the essays of Dr.

Bernard Pyron on transformational Marxism for many insights here.

The odd thing about the beginning of Dispensationalism is that its founders claimed that 'the Bible doesn't make sense without their system; God brought us along to explain the 2 programs and make sense of it.'

For some of you, this may be odd outright for the mere reason that it only makes sense that the Bible would have its own way of being coherent; we ought to be able *to find self-organization* within it. So you might say the true fault of the founders was not to find those statements or passages. Because of that, they believed they were 'anointed' to declare how it was organized.

But what Dispensationalism did, for whatever reason, was to break the meaning of early Acts about the throne of David. My point here is, after all that has been discussed in this study, that if you break that (deny it), you have pretty much broken the whole thing, and that was also Marxism's goal.

Dispensational asserted that there were really 2 programs in the Bible, Israel and the people of faith in the Gospel, and they were essentially different on every feature, but they 'carried' forward to the end, even though they might disappear from the picture for a while. Sometimes at the end, it is said that Israel ends up with its land, and Christians end up in heaven, and no answer is given about those who are both.

So now this 2nd force existed to break the meaning of early Acts. Now, they didn't state that as their purpose but they operated that way, altering all the meaning of the passages to preserve 2 programs. Christ could be talking very smoothly and directly about something, but all of a sudden start saying things about 'another program at another distant time.'

At this point several very curious things started emerging. One was the regular denial that there would was a new or faith-based "Israel" as found in the NT. Here we come very close in operations: Marxism denies a god, specifically who would be the basis of rights of man; Dispensationalism simply denies this new Israel feature in the NT.

It then started to insult the person who would refer to a 'spiritual' version of Israel, but also of many other 'themes, motifs and images' (--F. Bruce). Given full NT chapters on the graduation from the elementary level of the Law to the maturity in Christ, it seems to me that the NT wants its people to be *spiritual*! We can't just use the term metaphorical or figurative about the series of 'new things that are now here' (Heb. 9:11). It is very important to see that they are mark of spiritual maturity.

Marxism also simply resorts to insult. It is what is known as psy-ops. There is no discussion. You are automatically an idiot if you differ with them. You probably can see the parallel to discussions about evolution—if there are discussions!

Dispensationalism then featured strained interpretations, over and over, to get its point across. As for the meaning of Acts 2-3, that point was that an ordinary-type kingdom of Israel was offered but refused by the resurrected Christ, and the whole plan was altered by the refusal. We now just operate in a dismal period of evangelism which was not really the plan, and the great kingdom of Israel will come back at the right time— although it will fail in the end in 1000 years. Some followers of this 'ism' are unable to sort out when and how 1000 years and forever are different.

There are many variations, but they all embrace the 2 programs.

There is always an exception, and in this case, you have probably heard the (correct) explanation that 'the Jews of Jesus time thought Messiah was coming to break the control of Rome over them so they could be a free country.' This is a curious fact that Dispensationalism agrees to. It is found in elementary level materials. But very little is done with it!

The parallel in Marxism is that Marxism admits it needs the money of capitalism to create a socialist state, which is a step toward a massive and miserable Marxist state, as KGB defector Bezmenov explains. And as Romanians or Venezuelans know.

Eventually in the 2000s or so, the accusation was made by Dispensationalism that its opponents were engaged in Replacement Theology. But this was only a way of avoiding discussion. The object was to guilt people for being anti-semitic. It was only a confusion of several issues, now all quite removed from the powerful assertions of early Acts.

The Disappearance and the Opposite

We can now come to a further stage in which the similarity between these two Isms are rather shocking. Marxism rewrites history. Think of Solzienitzen's famous line: "The future is clear; it is the past that keeps changing."

I recently came across a line that *1984* was Orwell's last novel, and that when he died a year later, he was working on deflecting criticism that *1984* was about the Marxist empire. Really? Or is that more re-writing?

Somehow from the late 19th century on, the integration of NT with its own history was shattered. The force which the Holford study had almost disappears from the tool box. Around the mid 1960s I recall a childhood memory in which a fundamentalist church leader was warned not to read Josephus' histories and he was told not interact with a friend who did. Like many Dispensational churches, the same group had completely worked out the future event sequence.

In my 1970s college years, the Dispensational college I attended was not much better. There were vague references to Josephus as a lexical aid, but nothing about what NT history was like.

One day it did come back by surprise. A novel, MASADA, and a matching NBC movie came out which made the *zealots* the heroes. This was celebrated as being quite an achievement by professors and others in futurist churches. Perhaps, they thought, people would finally realize the reality of the Bible and the 'miracle' of Israel (they were really pointing to modern Israel). Thus the mass-suicide of the last of the zealots at Masada became iconic. This would complete a Marxist-like 'transformation' of a concept into its opposite.

In a way, I can see why a media company would want to subvert the apostolic doctrine of the enthroned King, but I don't know if they were conscious of it. What I do know, however, is that the Christian and futurist Trinity cable network TBN showed EXODUS regularly as its Sunday night movie. This movie's heroes are atheist terrorists seizing a ship to take Jews to Palestine. In a French movie with a similar theme, they are Marxists.

The relation of the NT to the destruction of Jerusalem, with all its overwhelming force to support the Christian belief that the Son would smash his enemies, was now a tool for the opposite. What was a force Paul once used to put Caesar in his place had now disappeared.

Truly, the situation now is not only that there is extremely rare knowledge that integrates the NT with the destruction of Jerusalem. There is almost no reason to know. The power of the kingdom in Acts is as marginalized by this as anything Marxism could ever dream. Transformational Marxism has won the day in educational and media efforts.

Perhaps most toxic of all is that the identity politics of Marxism won. All of its categories are about race or gender or class. Right to the present day, transformational Marxism continues to approve or disapprove on the basis of these things no matter what contradiction comes up. When the Bay Area authorities recently decided to change school names to avoid 'whiteness,' they changed one school named after Diane Feinstein, because she is *white*. Neither her socialist beliefs nor her gender mattered on that one.

By insisting on 2 disjointed programs at work in the Bible, one of them based on a race-nation, Dispensationalism has accomplished the same confusion and contradiction in its own way. A further similarity. At the end of the previous chapter, I gave three reasons why people left Europe that have nothing to do with the white racism claimed by the NYT's 1619 Project. It is utter paradox that futurist eschatology has nearly the same preoccupation with a race-nation, of another variation.

But now let's leave all this disintegration behind, and *integrate* the NT with its own history.

Integrating NT History

This is a concise coordinated statement about Luke-Acts, Jesus' Prophecy and the 'Great Revolt,' (aka Jewish War) from my initial research for a master's degree.

The expression 'Great Revolt' is used about the events of 66+ because of the simmering revolutionary situation all through the century.

We will first review the basic action of the war, then the Matthew section of chs. 21-25 about it, and finally the much-more detailed references in Luke to it.

Revolt may have been simmering in Judea for some time, ever since the challenge to Antiochus Epiphanes in the Greek period. There were regular discussions of revolt from that time on. In the Roman period, there was a 'pivoting' tolerance of Judaism; as long as Roman insiginia was displayed intact, the area's religions could do as they like. The maniacal Herod, who built up the Temple complex, introduced another element to the tension: a half-Jew who spent the country into debt with his paranoia about both Romans and Jews. The ongoing cost of the temple he built was not at all the glorious place of worship Judaism envisioned from its prophets, but it was better than 100 years earlier. And the longer it stood, the more zealots dreamed of using it as a fortress. Hold that thought.

Revolt spilled out during the Augustine census of 6 AD. The leader was Judas the Galilean. Remember that location (Galilee) for the duration of this account. Revolt simmered all through this time. An insurrection had occurred in Jerusalem, simultaneous to Jesus' ministry there.

At the end of Acts, getting close to the major outbreak of 66, a Roman administrator thought Paul was an Egyptian who started a revolt, 21:38. This kind of revolt was probably a regional attempt to pull Judea, Idumea and Nabatea into an alliance to break up Roman control. There were also other attempts to do so.

But it was a seizure of temple taxation money for Roman use which burst the dike in 66. The outcry began in the Galilean district and the Roman reprisal was a new thing: the burning of whole villages, in a 'sweep.'

In Jerusalem, it was a signal to seize areas and use them as fortresses of independence. Most accounts say there were 3 at first. Another Judas, Simon Bar-Giora and John of Gischala were section leaders, and John's area began to take the temple. It was odd that there would be a lack of cooperation, but John battled his way to become the sole leader. Rabbi Dennis Prager says of the overall event: "We destroyed ourselves."

Rome's general Vespasian was leading the encircling of Jerusalem (Lk 19:41), until there was a near-fracture of Rome itself in 68, when the seizure of Jerusalem paused. Vespasian did not come back; he became emperor. He sent his son Titus back to finish the task. The interruption was a boon to the zealots, and also allowed many Christians to escape to Pella in Jordan to safety.

Titus returned in 69, and in August of 70, on the same week of the year as the destruction of the temple in 586 BC, he was going to finish it off. The final months were full of pathetic conditions of poverty, starvation, cannibalism of children. Titus meant to preserve the Temple, but a fire was started and it was impossible to save. Josephus adds some unusual features to the final scenes: a voice from heaven, combined with a sword in the air overhead sweeping over the place; an extraordinary heat and roaring from the Temple itself; voices from the Temple saying 'We have departed; etc. He cites accounts of each of these from interviews which appear to be plausible.

About a thousand fighters with some of their families escaped to Masada where they repeated a stand and Josephus was among them, still as a priest and captain. When Rome succeeded with an earthworks ramp to gain control, there was a mass suicide, to deprive the Romans of the boast of capturing them. Then about 10 were left in one incident with Josephus among the 10. One was drawn by lots to end the others, but Josephus fled when he was not drawn and surrendered to the Roman army.

Over 1 million people had died in the destruction of the city. It is one of the classic accounts of antiquity.

Jesus' prophecy (Mt. 24, Mk. 13, Lk. 19&21) is about the calamity of AD 66. It obviously weighs heavily on his heart, Lk. 23:29. The appeal of Christ and the apostles to their people was for them to become missionaries of the Gospel of justification by Christ's righteousness, as Paul did. That was God's messianic plan all along, but also was a sane solution to the mistake of confrontation with Rome.

By and large, Israel did not follow, and Judaizers harassed Christians in their endeavors, and agitated the arrangement with Rome, and supported at least 3 freedom-fighting 'messiahs' in the 60s. This is why Jesus' prophecy (same passages) has such immediate and direct warnings about having to evacuate Jerusalem and Israel. Why would you have to worry about escaping for your life…on a Sabbath? Because of a police-state 'purifying' the land of Levitical law-breaking.

Finally, Christians expected a 2nd global and ultimate appearance of Christ on the heels of Daniel's desolating disaster of AD 66, but God had other plans about that, to save even more people. This means passages in Thessalonian letters, so vividly written in the 40s about what was coming, no longer have specific application. They are still generally encouraging about the final victory of Christ, of course, as is Revelation, which was also written before the Jewish War. But much of the debate about specifics has missed has what happened historically.

The best recent *non-scholarly* treatment of this I'm aware of is J. Zens, "The time of great affliction" SEARCHING TOGETHER, Fall-Winter 2005, p47+.

Jesus and the Decisive Generation
The following pages are a shot at summarizing Matthew 21-25 and inter-referring it to many other passages. Quite a bit is happening in that generation, to that generation, and because of that generation's decisions. This generation is the people alive and in front of Jesus, however, we have to keep in mind that at the time of the writing of Mt 21-25, the view is to the upcoming generation.

This last point distinguishes those who knew him in an ordinary sense, and those who realizes later through the preaching of the apostles that very extraordinary business had taken place—that God was in Christ, etc, as 2 Cor 5 says. Because God had completed redemption in Christ, there was now a new message and actually a "new creation" for all mankind and all of its religions to reckon with.

The Ride on the Colt
Obviously it was not "the" new creation coming at the end of the world. But somehow it made a statement here in *this* world. Which is precisely why we should start with the colt of Mt 21. Riding on that colt, was a statement that the kingdom of God was here, but in this form that was at once harmless (to the powers that be) *and* revolutionary. It was 'by faith' but also "demolishing strongholds."

Let's list the paragraphs or scenes of Mt 21-25 (using NIV captions):

The Triumphal Entry
Jesus at the Temple—Cleansing and the Children
The Fig Tree Withers
The Authority of Jesus Questioned
The Parable of the Two Sons
The Parable of the Tenants
The Parable of the Wedding Banquet
Paying Taxes to Caesar
Marriage at the Resurrection
The Greatest Commandment

Whose Son is the Christ?
Seven Woes at the Teachers of the Law
Signs of the End of the Age
The Day and Hour Unknown
The Parable of the Ten Virgins
The Parable of the Talents
The Sheep and the Goats

Jesus had to bring things to a head and make Jerusalem/Israel decide about him. We know this from the biting Parable of the Tenants, but it does not start there. The leaders are indignant about the songs to Jesus, and one line has been kept going by the children: "Hosanna (save us) to the Son of David." They try to obligate him to have them stop. But it was the right song!

Judaim's authorities were anxious about hearing reference to a 'son of David' Messiah, because Rome could react harshly. Yet the meaning of Christ about the 'son of David' was not that of the zealots. This frames the enthronement (the resurrection as the enthronement on David's throne) a couple months later.

He curses a fig tree the next morning for having all the leaves it should (it looked right from a distance) but no fruit. How symbolic is that!

So all questions about Christ come down to his authority. The leaders never did close the case of John, so Jesus says he has the same authority as John. This continues into the next because the "sinners" were receiving the kingdom of God and righteousness but the leaders were not.

That's what sets up the Parable of the Tenants. There has to be fruit. The tenants parable is the case where the workers figure the operation is theirs. The worker, in any job, doesn't know the next thing coming that the owner has to adapt to. They are supposed to produce. But these workers think the operation is theirs.

The remotely-managed grow operation here demands payment and gets none. Messengers are even killed. Then the son is sent and killed. So the vineyard is given to "a people" who will produce its fruit. While it is the same word for the nations, Jesus has just expressed things the same way that Paul strains to reach: a group, a people, a community who produces the fruit of the kingdom of God (and pays the owner!). It is not defined by race or lineage, but by honest work for the reign of God.

Caution: Falling Rock

Let us now note one minor "prop" in the overall message of Mt 21-25: the stone. That son who came and was rejected is also seen as a *cornerstone* for building a new building. So now we have a *new people* and a *new building* side by side. If that sounds familiar it is because it is how Paul described the new 'gathering' or 'ecclesia' or church

92

(before "church" was a word): a group that produced, and a building or temple. Peter has the same thing in I Pet. 2.

But again something very hard is said. The same stone just mentioned will fall upon others and this will crush them. The curiosity here is that the subject of carved or shaped stones will come up again shortly in the section: no stone of the temple will be left on top another, in a very short time.

The Wedding Banquet parable has some similar statements. The servants of a king announcing a wedding are killed just for announcing it. It will also mention an army coming against a city and demolishing it (22:7), however, that's only the halfway point. Someone from the demolished city eventually comes to the wedding but assumes they can come in wearing ordinary clothes. This will not do, and he is tied up and thrown out of the party for his presumptiveness. Jesus is telling Israel that it must be clothed in Christ's righteousness. It can't come in on its own terms.

Jesus is not inciting a conflict with Rome; taxes must be paid. The ride on the colt was obviously non-threatening in terms of civil unrest. He is not setting aside law but he knows how to express the most fundamental law 'upon which everything else hangs.'

He wasn't finished with that question about David's son, and this brings us to a point where we can organize certain things. He is the Son of David as prophesied. He has a kingdom but it will not conflict with Rome. He expects fruit for the kingdom and will crush those who do not produce; watch out for falling rock!

He then gives seven condemnations of Judaism. Not least is the rejection of God's messengers, which had already been a theme in a couple parables. (Mt 21-25 is very cohesive!). The punishment for this would fall on *this generation*. (23:36-37). Therefore the house (the national sense of coherence and purpose) is desolate. (The temple itself would be soon.) The leaders would not "get" (understand) him until they sang what the children sang.

If it's not clear yet, "this generation" (the subject of these parables) would see the temple torn down and a huge calamity in the city. It was one of those things that was so shocking to hear, the disciples couldn't respond right away. They knew of Dan. 9 (and Jesus would make one decisive, clear statement about that), and how a desolation was foretold. But was it really now, really this amazing temple? So they kicked it around and asked him a bit later.

They knew that Dan. 9's 490 years would come to an end very soon, and certainly it was shaping up to be a unique generation they were heading into. It was. It was a *decisive* generation.

A Messy-anic War

The worst thing about what was coming was the high risk of deception. It was going to be a messianic war against Rome, but that was the problem. The nation would be asked by several messiahs to follow them and fight. The end of the world would be after that, but there would be quite a catastrophe in Israel before that.

If you go back to the issue about the taxes to Caesar, you must put yourselves in the people's shoes. They had now heard twice in parable form that there would be a traumatic ending to what they knew as Israel. They wanted to treat their religion as something that was for their sake; he was telling them it was about to produce new wine, new fruit that he wanted. They would come to a "wretched end" and their "city burned."

Shouldn't they then fight for their freedom against this happening? Why should they keep paying taxes to those who oppress them? That is why the next question about taxes comes out. That revolt was what they wanted to do. That was the messianic dream of the next generation coming up. Jesus was in his own categories: he neither validated Judaism nor upset the Herodians who were comfortably nestled in Rome's lap.

It would be a ragged generation. Christians would be hated in Israel and in all nations. Yet the Gospel would be spread to all nations too.

But the signal to Christians in Jerusalem to clear out was the surrounding armies and the use of the temple by one of these imposter 'messiahs.' At that point, Jesus said, get out of Judea. For you would either be killed by maniac messianic troops and their Sabbath police, or by Roman ones trying to silence the land. So again, don't let your fears get you and don't be deceived by the 'messiahs.' For one thing, when the Son of Man does come, it was to be a clear as an end-to-end sheet-lightning flash. It would not be a 'movement' building secretly until it could find a flash-point.

In the summary of the revolt above, I mentioned that the attack on Jerusalem was paused by Vespasian because of a political earthquake back in Rome. This was an act of mercy on Christians who should have left Jerusalem already. The sign to leave was the new of 'encirclement.' But there were those who tried to stay, to perhaps wrap up business affairs, to try to persuade other family members to leave, etc. Wars are messy. Fortunately more escaped the city due to the pause.

He then explains the end of the world, and there are some similarities to the destruction of Israel, but the details of the ordeal in Judea are over with. The similarities are in matters like readiness or denial. The believers should be busy at tasks of the kingdom and taking care of the needy, because the needy are like tokens of Christ who need to be taken care of.

Mt. 21-25 has been summarized as far as the issues before Israel in that generation. We will now survey Luke about the war.

Luke: Jesus Answers the Zealot Revolutionaries and Rome's Questions

There is a need to 'hear' all of Luke in its historic setting. Luke's portrayal of Jesus is especially informed by Paul, with whom Luke traveled, and who needed to be cleared of any connection with revolutionary activity in Judea. This essay will skim Luke and show those places that speak to the problem of the Galilean revolutionaries or zealots.

Luke's gospel's side-glances about the war tends to run *early* in the narrative. There are sayings and teachings that come earlier than in the other 2 synoptics (Mt, Mk and Lk are the *synoptics*: same *point of view* of the events, unlike John).

When he sends out the 70 missionaries, he speaks of their treatment in the same language as when believers will be out and about in Judea leading up to the destruction of Jerusalem. He is early on that. Both Matthew and Luke use the same language for both events (the mission trip and the destruction of the city); among other things this shows the direct, present meaning of Christ.

The placement of the transfiguration is early: ch 9th of 24, vs Mt's 16th of 28 chapters. He already announces then that they will see the kingdom come. Likewise, in speaking of the destruction of Jerusalem of 66+, Luke gets to it very early. Mt 24 and Mk 13 are both late in the story in each of their cases. Their location matches where they are proportionately, about 4/5 the way through the total.

The most revolutionary-leaning part of Israel was the Galilean area. In 6 AD, or the 'time of the census' as Gamaliel calls it in Acts 5, Judas the Galilean led a revolt which was put down. The area then has that notoriety all through the gospel accounts. The reputation is not one of being backward or 'hick,' but of being more vocal in revolt against Rome. Down in Jerusalem, they were sure Messiah would not come from the Galilee. He didn't, really, being born in Bethlehem, but he lived there and there is a reason why he made an appeal to this volatile group. He was trying to save his nation.

In 12, he warns the country that he will not bring peace; he will be a thing that divides Israel. It is one thing to say this when it is unified, and quite another to say this when it is favoring revolutionaries, which was the case. These revolutionary zealots expect supernatural help from God to battle Rome, and Jesus has a very low opinion of all that. He then says his generation must interpret what is going on: a storm is coming. Israel is going to be devasted by a punishing army (explained a bit later), but this is set in the final paragraph of 12 as a matter of being on the way to court: Israel should settle before getting there, to that 'court.'. Jesus uses the expression 'seek the things of peace' here and uses it about the conflict with Rome in ch 19. He means that Israel should be joining his mission, not the (military) mission of the zealots.

Ch. 13 follows immediately with an incident in which some of the Galilean rebels were reported killed by Pilate. The storm was coming. Some people died when a tower in Jerusalem collapsed, and he warned that the whole city would die likewise without repentance. We know that everyone is mortal and going to die, but this was a specific, concrete warning to Jerusalem. The revolutionaries wanted a place to operate out of in Jerusalem, and Jesus has some pointed remarks about them in ch 14 (below).

So he has come into a time in which zealous religious revolutionaries are on a mission, and his intent is to derail them. They are playing on ancient and recent 'revelations' of a victorious warrior king endorsed by God, and whipping up the people based on this. They are calling out that a 'messiah' has been spotted 'in the inner rooms' of the temple or 'out in the desert.'

He's just getting started. He continues in 13 with the fig tree as a parable. He is "the man" who appeals to the owner for a year of delay before cutting it down. That delay year is the generation after his crucifixion, who was appealed to over and over to join the mission of the Gospel.

13 ends with express sorrow for the place. Sorrow for its treatment of the prophets, and because it will be devasted. The house (an icon for the whole national identity; like '*dar*' in Arabic) is *already* declared desolate. It's nearly 40 years in advance! They would only understand him if they sang Ps 118 of him. That's the cornerstone psalm.

In 14, there is a connection between sayings about the upcoming battle and being salt of the land (cp. to Mt 5). He says it is foolish for 10K to fight 20K, but of course the #s were far worse in the upcoming war. But notice a technical term in v32 'terms of peace' (*ta pros eirenen*). This will be the exact same phrase he uses to speak to Israel in ch 19. He had said in the Sermon on the Mount that they were salt of the land ('*ges*' often means the land of Israel, not the whole earth). That is, if they would do things like not confront soldiers, but help them. Roman soldiers! Quite a different tack than the zealots, wearing their hidden '*sicarii*' swords. But if salt loses its power, it is tossed. So salt/preserving has to do with the previous: with not following the zealots or Judaizers into conflict with Rome.

But he had also mentioned the failed building of a tower, and the last tower mentioned in Luke was 13:4. It was a symbol of what would happen to the revolution; it would collapse under unrealistic planning.

In 17, he laments that this generation would be as mindless about what was coming as in the days of the flood, and Sodom. Dan 9 had in fact said the end (TBD) would be 'like a flood,' too.

In 19 comes a warning that parallels Mt's parables of the vineyard and wedding, even though Luke will include the vineyard in 20. The servants who had done poorly with the money were to be killed.

19 of course includes the 1st paragraph on the devastation coming on Israel who refused the 'terms of peace.' As a reminder, this term was used back in 14:32 about negotiating with a huge approaching army.
Embankments, surrounding, hemming in, people dashed to the ground, children too, the place torn down. All this was coming upon that generation, on whom was imputed all the abuse of the prophets, because the prophets and

their times 'longed to see the days of the Son.'

19:46 contains an unusual detail. When cleansing the temple, Jesus says 'you have made it a den of robbers' (*leistes*). There are other terms for thieves, but this one has to do with rebels, brigands, insurrectionists. He was saying exactly what would happen to the temple: it would be made a rebellious HQ. That would seem to be the 'abomination that desolates,' a phrase from Dan 9 that originally was expressed as 'the *rebellion* that desolates' in Dan 8.

In 20:18 there are stones that are fallen on, and people break into pieces. Then there are stones that *fall on people*, and they are crushed. Coincidental imagery? He had just used them in 19:44. Both of them.

This may explain why his answer about the coming destruction uses the same imagery, 21:6. The 3rd time is a charm, so to speak. In 12, the same language about persecution and rejection was used as about the 70 who were sent; the same kinds of conditions. As for people, or at least believers, in Jerusalem, they were given a signal to leave. The punishment coming (if we needed clarification) was to fulfill *everything* written--in old covenant terms and conditions, is the idea. It was the end of that, the end of that era.

V25 is where Luke leaves the Judean setting behind, and speaks of the global events of the return of Christ, expected right after the destruction of Jerusalem.

Finally in 23:28, the most powerful and selfless thing he does is to tell those in his wake, on his way to death, to look after themselves and their children because of the awful things about to happen. "You daughters and your children." The time coming for them (ie, that generation) will be so bad, it will be dreaded as the end of the world. Jesus was *betrayed* when the tree was green. The public had decided to *spare* one of the revolutionaries! The tree (Israel) will be cut down, and then guess what men will do?

He'd already told them.

The Galileans
But let us back up at least to the point where Jesus called his twelve and we notice that they were mostly Galileans. But even that is not the point. He was also called a Galilean, and his family brings him up there even though he was born in Bethlehem because of the census requirement to turn in your information where you were born.

The Galilean area had a more vocal crowd. The misgiving about associating with them was not that they were uneducated or backward (cp. 'hillbillies') but that they were more inclined to revolt and risk the balance of administration in Judea.

In the same year as the census, and probably due to it, a certain figure arose, Judas the Galilean, and attempted to whip up popular revolt. This was referenced by Rabbi Gamaliel in his advice not to punish the apostles severely in Acts 5. Yet even though Judas' revolt died out, others popped up and one NT background book title is ISRAEL IN REVOLUTION 6-73 CE because the waves continued to come. It was a holy war, or rather, a holy *revolt*.

It was this crowd which was also very ripe for a 'messiah' who would work in coordination with them. This is found in other literature of the time: scrolls, apocalyptic writings, etc. A final, climactic, eschatological war is expected to resolve all of this and restore what Israel had at one time. Pages of OT prophets also fed this: something was due to happen after the punishing exile to Babylon. The readers didn't seem to notice the visions kept bursting beyond the normal dimensions of life.

So we should now look at Jesus' selection of his twelve and notice that for the most part he intentionally appealed to this group of people. He risked the fact that he might have a Judas (note the patriotism of the name—a name based on your country--as well as the echo of the rebel mentioned by Gamaliel), and even before the betrayal, Judas had expressed the gripe that money to anoint Jesus for his burial could have gone to help poor people. He also risked having those who might be violent. His Judas had the nickname Iscariot, from the 'sicari' or assassination-dagger which was short and curved so that Roman soldiers could not detect it under a Judean's usual clothing.

It was specifically to these people that Jesus introduced that the Christ was not going to be their hero-conqueror but a sacrifice for sins. This theme begins very early in the gospels. His mother names him as such, a "Joshua" who saves from sins. John the Baptist announces him as a sacrificial lamb, which is hardly an icon for counter-attacking strength and leadership. One of his first miracles is a brilliant proof of divine authority to forgive sins: a two-part 'bargain' with an audience that doubts he can *either* heal *or* has such authority is treated to the healing as proof of the other. He explains the cause and effect of being forgiven of sin as a debt to both Judaism's leaders and a woman in huge moral debt early in his teachings, so that the leaders could see the power of what he was offering in himself—in his own sacrificial life, which would be a 'ransom' for many.

And then we come to an extremely interesting obstacle to all this. In spite of all the ground laid, when it actually comes to explaining to the twelve that he will be slaughtered in Jerusalem and then resurrected, they are clueless and speechless. This is referenced many times in Matthew, Mark, and Luke although only slightly in John. They have no idea what he is talking about and don't want to ask him about it. This wasn't the "Christ" they were expecting. Nor their Galilean friends.

Even Peter blurts out that this will not happen, when first realizing what he is hearing. "Never, Lord!" Yet he did not have in mind 'the things of God.'

Mission vs revolution
This blockage will be eventually solved by the Spirit's work and Jesus' teaching between the Resurrection and Pentecost. But let us just note for now that Jesus apparently chose these twelve because they would have this problem. He deliberately wanted twelve Galileans with this inherent problem in Judaism to try to influence the generation that was so far headed for a collision with the Roman empire's administration of its state. He wanted the twelve to be examples to their Galilean friends that there was a completely different direction to take on all the questions that rebels had taken. And that all this was due to a different "Christ" than theirs. At risk were the level of stability that Israel had at the time; at least the

leadership could speak of their 'place and temple' that might be lost if there was unrest. In a few decades they would be lost.

Jesus had no vision of a restored Davidic state to bring to Israel but he did see that generation as the one to launch the mission that the OT prophets had envisioned of the knowledge of the Lord spread to the nations. The launch was successful. By the 60s the new mission was stronger outside Judea than inside.

This vision and appeal to Israel is why we find so much attention in Luke to the revolt and the Galileans. In Acts 1 there is the last impulse remaining in the apostles to ask about Israel's kingdom, and it is swallowed up in the *mission*. The kingdom is to be no concern to them, but they would receive the power of the Spirit for the *mission*. There is no mention of the kingdom in the Acts 13:47 quote of Isaiah about the mission, and the fallen tent of David in Acts 15 that has been put back up is the mission to the nations.

Perhaps the best place to leave off is the vision of the Seed and stump in Isaiah 6. It says that the land would be ruined *a second time*, but the Seed would sprout from the remaining stump. It is hard to find a simpler summary.

Jesus specifically reached out to Galilean rebels to turn them away from their plan, and to the mission to the nations. This was all documented by Luke so that Roman administrators would know that they did not have a double-agent zealot in Paul. The enthroned King was going to have a kingdom that went in a new direction.

Impact

You can watch my documentary BE CAREFUL WHAT YOU WISH FOR and you will see that English society was impacted by knowing how these NT things integrated. The mob revolution lost all its charm, through the explanation of the disaster of the revolt.

But we have progressed. The reforms which took place and gave us the US Constitution have been violated in the 2020 election, while the synthetic reason for the revolution of that same year (Black Lives Matter) has regressed to the point of contradiction and senselessness. Climate change is now a "race issue." 1984-style censorship of truth is now pandemic.

The integrated power of the material presented here will hopefully overthrow the madness of the Left in the West once more. It is no good to depict a world which has no King, or which will have one some future day that is irrelevant to us.

Additional Features

The Strange Case of
the Translation of Acts 3:21

Using biblegateway.com's list of translation options, I found that half of translations have 1, wrecklessly changed heaven from being the subject of the sentence to an indirect object (a location) in 3:21, and 2, provided a 'constraint' type of verb (to stay, to keep, to remain), where none is justified.

The idea is that heaven is personified, almost like in the parable of the prodigal (I have sinned against heaven) and is holding the universe's greatest reception, and loudest.

The BAG and Analytical lexicons show that the few uses of 'dexesthai' mean to receive as in a reception. To shorten this you could say 'honor'. There is one *satirical* use of the term in 2 Cor 7 about the 'super-apostles' and how willing the Corinthians were to host them with honors, but how much Paul had to fight for his place among them.

All of which is very fishy. We should be seeing the continuation here of the Royal ascension psalms--the King has been enthroned (for ex. Ps 24, 89, 93, 95, 96, 97, 98, 99, 103, 110, 45, 47, and all of those who dwell 'above' are in full voice in welcoming and singing about him. Heb 12 gives us a 'list' of what is going on in heaven--as we speak--and Rev 5-7 provides the lyrics and sound effects (the sound of a mighty waterfall).

So what on earth is this translation flaboodle about?

I can only guess that the translators that went with a restraint concept assumed that the reader would think of it in terms of 'Christ would be *the only one* who would be honored so exclusively; heaven would hold him *alone* in such an exalted place.' But in fact, many, many people, thanks to the misconceptions of futurism have thought that it meant 'God is keeping Christ in heaven now because the church and its mission was a total afterthought and He is going to be sent down later to set up a kingdom on earth through the race-nation Israel that is expressed through the prophets' writings. After all, the rebuke not to think about such a kingdom in Acts 1 is not the same as dismissing it.'

How We Get Back to Meaning in Life
A universal story

I hope you will 'hear' this story long enough to see that 'get back to meaning' is the most important expression here. It is the story of a person who had, by all accounts, the most meaningful start in life.

There was a man *who wore himself out fighting for what he thought was the meaning in life and for his people. They had become poor, occupied, ruined, relocated, and precariously close to starvation. They used to be on top. They had a shining city* *on a hill, a mountain fort. But now it was run by a capricious madman. There used to be something that bound them all together but it was lost and dry. People were either leaving the tradition or beating those who left. It was a pretty ugly situation.*

Almost all of us start life in a place where there is significant meaning or even tradition to what we do and are. Such is the nature of human life. Coming in along underneath that launch in life is a conception that it will always be that way.

But things happen to us in life and much of it is altered. We may even go back to those things we had started with and find they are gone or simply not the way we remembered and we have to abandon our search there.

For this man, an unusual thing happened. I mentioned that he actually fought to preserve these things. One day, he was out doing that and punishing some of the people who had left, and he was stopped. Not by his own conscience, nor by doubts about his tradition. A person stopped him, right in the road, and this person had been gathering his own followers around him, specifically by saying the old ways were not going to be meaningful as they once were and something new had come.

Now, keep in mind, this was not the kind of meeting where the man had any choice. It was not going to be a debate about the old ways. Instead, this new person had special powers, and was sort of taking over control of the guy. Why? Because he was aggressive and was outspoken, and the person who stopped him planned on using those features. But that would come later after some retraining.

First, however, came the realization that the old ways really were not as meaningful as he had thought growing up. Then came some grief, as he realized that he had really damaged a lot of people by being the enforcer of the old ways. Finally came the new vision for this man, that he was actually going to be sent all over the known world to help others see how it was that we get back to meaning, and to launch many others with the same message.

Now, we must understand here, that any one who had been told that he was going to go all over the world with a message like that would come across as conceited or goofy like a television evangelist. But the man soon learned that it was not like this at all. The reason this new message would go all over was because of the very type of message itself.

It was the kind of message which no longer proposed that we simply switch from one kind of object in our usual world to another, and say 'I'm really into this.' That would simply ignore the fact that the next object of attention was also finite and would fail one day to provide. That also put a lot of value on you as the seeker, as though your seeking had no weaknesses or mistakes to it. That is not a good plan.

The person I have been talking about is Saul, later Paul.

This is a person who lived in 1st century Judea in the shadow of Jesus Christ. When he grew up, he was taught that his people would be a special race and refresh the whole world. He was also taught that he was at the end of a cycle or segment of history when an age of such revitalizing the world was about to take place under a fantastic leader, even a manifestation of God, and that it would involve the ancient shrine his people always had.

He was very vigorous in pursuing this, and for what it is worth, he could trace his lineage back to one of the 12 original brothers that founded his people. He could actually 'talk' his way through the custody of ancestry, without a computer or internet.

Back at the beginning, they said there was a promise that in the seed of the founding father would be a blessing for all nations. In this case, 'seed' meant his offspring. The thing was, the descendants all thought it was themselves taken as a group. And he thought the blessing was their law, their collection of rules, most of which reminded them about being separate.

Like I said, Paul was kind of taken charge of as a person. He was taken out into the desert for several years. And this was to reformulate what he thought.

The thing about this reshaping or redoing of his thought was what it meant about the seed. Everything Paul had been raised to think was about the people as a race or nation. But Paul knew that it was all in a pretty miserable state. The only thing Paul knew to do was to fight for it—for its purity, its *loyalty. To purge out half-interested people. To Paul, it was either that, or there was no point. And he found himself saying there was no point very quickly during this interception.*

But then in the desert he was shown something else. And it changed everything. He was shown that the Seed was Christ and what had taken place in him, not the nation.

Now this is not much, except that Paul had everything about meaning in his life riding on what he had grown up with. And through his life, he learned that it was all falling apart badly.

But there was something else about being out in the desert in this case. It was that the person who was telling him that the Seed was Christ and was a gift for all nations, was the same person who had taken Moses 'out in the desert'. The person who had made that promise, back when his people was an extremely tiny and ragged band roving across the ancient middle east, was now saying it meant something as broad as the oceans.

Something else happened when the meaning of it all came back in Christ. The meaning of everyone now came back. For the message was something that would automatically spread. Because everyone on earth was connected to it. He now realized how his people were indeed a conduit to all the nations, and that would link each of them to the purpose of God, merely by hearing it. It was already set for them. But actually anyone who repeated the message would spread the blessing.

It wasn't something his people had to bring about, and it would not come about by their harsh enforcement of it. Nor would all their effort to keep separate accomplish anything. It would not be confined to one place. It was meant to go to all nations, to the ends of the earth.

The Seed, which had come from his people, had been given a title higher than any figure on earth, in this age and the next. An event had just taken place, also in his country, bestowing the Seed with that honor.

"In your Seed, all the nations of the earth will be blessed." That "Seed" had come, and had accomplished justification for us from our sins. It was about thinking of sins as a debt, and the debt had been paid by someone else.

This was exceptional because it linked everyone to the very first promise to that forefather. But Paul realized also that this 'forefather' thing was a limiting expression. He really should be saying, and did say, that he was the father of all who believe, not just his ancestors' forefather. The same good news about the Seed and the nations had been preached to Abraham, and when Abraham believed the debt of his sins was dropped.

That meant it went back even further. As soon as evil entered this world by a deliberate mistake of Adam and Eve, God announced the coming of a Seed. That Seed would be injured somewhat but would crush the Enemy of mankind--and of goodness--who had led them into darkness.

The link really was all the way back to the beginning of time and was 'big' enough, as high concepts go, to help everyone get back to meaning in life. They now had something to believe, but they also now had something to do.

Some years after the reformulation, he was gathered with people mostly from his race, but living two countries away from the homeland. Knowing he had just been in the main city, they asked him if he had anything encouraging to say. Talk about the best question you could ask! All the reports were pretty dismal. It had become meaningless. There were rumors the whole place could go up in smoke.

He told them the whole shape of their history and destiny had come in Christ, and that things were actually quite upbeat. He said it was really fine news—not what the country was like, but these events in Christ. And then he read them one of their old writings, that in this message was the chance for them to be lights to the nations. No one could believe that there was an echo of that old saying about the Seed's blessing for nations. They all knew that line had come from the forefather. Yet there it was, routed through this one Seed.

Some talked to him for hours. Others invited him back for the following weekly meeting. Some were really upset.

Because we all get back to the one meaning of life this same way. These were real events, and each of our own life-stories, also in that history—not in fiction--ties back to this one Seed. Other explanations of meaning arise to distract us or confuse us about the enthroned Seed.

The 'Anothen' Realm

We must be born 'anothen;'
we belong to a city 'anothen';
the kingdom is 'anothen.'

There are at least two problems when trying to understand the kingdom of God. 1, the "location" of the term 'anothen.' 2, the confusion caused by using 'again' to translate 'anothen' in expressions like 'you must be born again.'

There is no confusion that the type of kingdom came as planned. The expression 'prepare the way for the Lord' had to do with a king moving around; John used it in the era of Christ to announce him.

Of course, there is all kinds of confusion from futurism about the kingdom because they immediately qualify the thing and seek to use the dull tools of 'spiritual' vs 'physical' as the only categories available.

The type of kingdom--and actually *the type of effect of* that kingdom--was always that it would be just a little above what we know as a government, but not be a government. All people, kings and commoners, were to be subject to it. Several centuries later, after the Reformation, the US founders would say that the minimal government they sketched could only work if the people in it were virtuous. If you understand that, you are very close.

The kingdom was empowered by the Gospel of God that, through the grace being shed abroad in Christ, a person would be willing to obey God. That may sound weak, but the same kingdom had the 'rod of iron'--that all subjects were on notice that they must pay homage to the Son or He would smash them.

There is nothing you need to know about the 2nd coming other than that. Most pursuit of information about the 2nd coming is prognostication and pretty tenuous.

So in Jn 3, a leader in Judaism is told that he needs to be born from above (which does have a way of being again, but not a human birth again), or else he can't see it. Now remember, this person knew Dan 2. He knew a kingdom was coming in Rome's time, and then there was all the amazing events of the nativity. But anyone could read Dan 2 and realize that the type of kingdom was unlike the previous: a growing mountain rather than a man-made statue which was poorly-conceived (weakest materials for the feet). The vision also introduced the Cornerstone that smashes things.

To clarify what is being born from above, Jesus explains the Gospel. That would be the Gospel that Futurism says doesn't exist until several years later when God goes plan B with Paul. This powerful concept is how the 'anothen' kingdom gets around.

The kingdom is *always* presented in *'just-beyond' or 'a little above'* terms. You don't fight for it with weapons. It has manifestations and imprints, but you can't see it in the normal sense. It is 'at hand.' It comes 'near you' and people come 'very close' to it. It's king is slaughtered but that's because the kingdom below it is subject to it, and accomplishing things as planned. The kingdom has an enthronement festival: it's the resurrection of Christ on David's throne, Acts 2. The kingdom is quaking with power, and when the apostles pray to understand why Judaism is rejecting them, they pray Ps 2 and the ground where they are shakes.

The letter of Hebrews is no different. The unshakeable kingdom is still full of life and of the festival of the enthronement of Christ and the joy and music of all previous believers, but it is not on this earth and not meant to be. It is for the new heavens and earth. Yet every day-- every moment--we draw hope from it and its victory over death.

Another important sense found in the lexical aids can tie this book and the 'universal story' about meaning all together: 'anothen' can mean 'from the beginning.' The Seed was from the beginning; he was the good news for a shattered world. But the Judaism of Christ's time, of Nicodemus, was concerned with and defined by what they were now. They were not reaching back to the actual roots *before* Abraham. Even in marriage, they wrangled about Moses' divorce law, but 'it was not that way from the beginning' answered Christ. That was the same limited reach.

Background Resources

Aune, D. "The Apocalypse of John and Graeco-Roman Revelatory Magic." 1987.

BBC. MASADA, documentary. 1980.

Beasley-Murray, G. JESUS AND THE FUTURE. 1956.

Berkhof, H. CHRIST AND THE MEANING OF HISTORY. 1966.

Bevenot, H. "Execratio Vastastionis," REVUE BIBLIQUE, 1936.

Bezmenov, Y. "Soviet defector on Marxist-Leninist practice." Youtube. 2020.

Bray, J. MATTHEW 24 FULFILLED.

Bright, J. THE KINGDOM OF GOD. 1953.

Brinsmead, R. "The Apocalyptic Spirit," VERDICT, Feb. 1981.

Same. "Justification By Faith and Eschatology" PRESENT TRUTH, 1974.

Same. "New Testament Eschatology," PRESENT TRUTH.

Bruce, F. THE THEMES, MOTIFS AND IMAGES OF THE OLD TESTAMENT FULFILLED IN THE NEW. 1970.

Bockmuel, K. MARXISM AND THE GOSPEL. 1975.

Cooper, B. AFTER THE FLOOD. 1995.

Cornfield, G, ed. JOSEPHUS: THE JEWISH WAR. 1982.

Cotter, G. "The Abomination of Desolation," CANADIAN JOURNAL OF THEOLOGY. 1957.

Crossan, J. JESUS; A REVOLUTIONARY BIOGRAPHY. 1995.

Davies, D. THE GOSPEL AND THE LAND. 1974.

Davies and Daube, eds. THE BACKGROUND OF THE NEW TESTAMENT AND ITS ESCHATOLOGY. 1964.

Diop, S. CIVILIZATION OR BARBARISM?

Ellis, E. PAUL'S USE OF THE OT. 1957.

Engels, F. THE PEASANT REVOLT.

ESI, Int'l. "Explaining Christianity to Chinese University Students."

Freyne, S. "Galilee—Jerusalem Relations According to Josephus' Life." 1987.

Gartner, B. COMMUNITY IN QUMRAN AND IN THE NEW TESTAMENT. 1965.

Gaston, L. NO STONE ON ANOTHER. 1970.

Grant, M. THE JEWS IN THE ROMAN ERA. @1970.

Hedges, C. AMERICA; THE FAREWELL TOUR. 2016.

Hengel, M. "Was Jesus A Revolutionary?" 1974.

Holford, G. THE DESTRUCTION OF JERUSALEM. 1835.

King, D. "Mark 13:24-27 and the Destruction of the Temple," REGENT COLLEGE THESES. 1979.

Lattourrette, K. HISTORY OF CHRISTIANITY. 1958.

Longenecker, R. BIBLICAL EXEGESIS IN THE APOSTOLIC PERIOD. 1975.

MacPherson, R. "Lutheran Political Resistance and the Magdeburg Confession 1550." HAUSVATER PROJECT, 2020.

Michener, J. THE SOURCE.

Middelmann, U. PRO-EXISTENCE. 1974.

Moore, G. JUDAISM. 1962.

Orwell, G. *1984*. 1949.

Paine, T. THE RIGHTS OF MAN. 1790.

Pentecost, D. THINGS TO COME. 1958.

Potok, C. WANDERINGS. 1978.

Pyron, B. "Dispensationalism and the Remant" essays at THEOLOGY FORUMS (general theology and Mid-Acts Dispensationalism folders) online. 2019-2020

Same. "Transformational Marxism" essays at THEOLOGY FORUMS (politics) online. 2019-2020

Rhoads, D. ISRAEL IN REVOLUTION, 6—74 CE. 1976.

Riggan   MESSIANIC THEOLOGY AND CHRISTIAN FAITH. 1967.

Ryrie, C. DISPENSATIONALISM TODAY.

Sanford, M. BE CAREFUL WHAT YOU WISH FOR documentary. 2020.

Same. "Christ's Victory Over the 'Elementary Principles of This World," SEARCHING TOGETHER. 1983.

Schaeffer, F. HOW SHOULD WE THEN LIVE? 1976.

Same. THE CHURCH AT THE END OF THE TWENTIETH CENTURY.

Schaff, P. HISTORY OF THE CHRISTIAN CHURCH. 1910.

Taylor, V. THE FORMATION OF THE GOSPEL TRADITION. 1964.

Thackeray, H. JOSEPHUS. 1928.

Thielicke, H. CHRIST AND THE MEANING OF LIFE. 1952.

Tyson, J. "The Gentile Mission and the Authority of Scripture." 1987.

Van Meter, D. "The Dating Game" (Revelation), SEARCHING TOGETHER, 2005.

Wright, G. GOD WHO ACTS. 1952.

Zens, J. "Identifying the Great Tribulation" SEARCHING TOGETHER. 2005.

Mr. Sanford *has an MCS in Christian Studies from Regent College, Canada, on Luke-Acts and the Jewish Revolt, as well as on Alexander's theory of design and creativity in connection with God. His effort in media has resulted in:*
contacting over 100 Christian film makers to use an archive for raising interest and investment in their mass media projects;

the documentary BE CAREFUL WHAT YOU WISH FOR on revolution and the background of his novel DESOLATED (MORE OF THE SAME);

the Cataclysm Infoboard program of geology interpretive displays;

6 *other novels and scripts;*

'book videos' for DESOLATED, THE NERVE, and
SENSELESS at Youtube;

he regularly works in an online outreach at theologyforums.com;

In the 1990s Mr. Sanford was invited to speak to the American
Association of Popular Culture on how the term 'nature'
changed in the 20th century.

He has been in ministry in Washington State, Beijing, Germany
and in Moldova in 2009, where he was unexpectedly present
during the anti-communist post-election uprising while helping
at a pastor's conference.

Interplans.net Studio can help you move a simple story concept
forward to complete form at an vetted archive for agents to
browse.

Made in the USA
Columbia, SC
20 June 2024